SHORT CUTS

INTRODUCTIONS TO FILM STUDIES

OTHER SELECT TITLES IN THE SHORT CUTS SERIES

POSTMODERNISM AND FILM

RETHINKING HOLLYWOOD'S AESTHETICS

CATHERINE CONSTABLE

WALLFLOWER

LONDON and NEW YORK

A Wallflower Press Book

Wallflower Press is an imprint of
Columbia University Press
Publishers Since 1893
New York, Chichester, West Sussex
cup.columbia.edu

Cover image: *Kill Bill: Vol. 1 (2003)* © *A Band Apart/Miramax*

A complete CIP record is available from the Library of Congress

ISBN 978-0-231-17455-8 (pbk. : alk. paper)
ISBN 978-0-231-85083-4 (e-book)

Columbia University Press books are printed on permanent and durable acid-free paper.
This book is printed on paper with recycled content.

Printed in the United States of America

p 10 9 8 7 6 5 4 3 2 1

CONTENTS

For my father, David Constable

A scientist by training and a great listener who has always been prepared
to discuss the nature of truth, life and the universe with me,
since I first started asking questions.

With love and thanks.

ACKNOWLEDGEMENTS

This is the first book I have written that is based on my teaching and so I must thank all the students who have taken my modules over the last decade or so, particularly Hollywood, Theories of the Moving Image, and, of course, the variously titled Postmodernisms. Thank you for asking great questions and for recommending wonderful films that were then incorporated into the modules! Particular thanks goes to those who team-taught with me on Hollywood, especially Ed Gallafent and Pete Falconer, who have profoundly influenced my thinking about *Kill Bill*. I also want to thank Adam Gallimore for providing me with a much-needed education in image capture! I have greatly benefitted from being able to try out elements of this book while it was still being written. Members of the Graduate Research Forum at King's College London were the first to hear chapter one and friends' and colleagues' kind reception of key ideas encouraged me to continue. Returning to writing has, as ever, involved considerable assistance from great friends, including Valerie Orpen's helpful contributions to chapter one and Rachel Jones' invaluable engagement with the postmodern theory explored across the book. Jane Worrall's meticulous editing has enhanced the whole and restored accuracy to my bibliography! I have been most touched by the help and support of my friends during times in which they have been very hard pressed. My family have had to grow accustomed to not seeing me at weekends and so my profound thanks to David and Iona for remaining entirely cheery and even enthusiastic about this project despite two months of neglect. Finally, back to my students – I hope this book will remind you of the modules that you enjoyed and that it succeeds in being both rigorous and fun.

Catherine Constable

June 2015

INTRODUCTION

The term 'postmodernism' in the title 'Postmodernism and Cinema' links together a particular historical period and a distinctive aesthetic style. It is therefore helpful to distinguish between postmodernity – an epoch defined by its relation to the modern – and postmodern aesthetics – the key stylistic features of postmodernist artworks. Both the historical and the aesthetic definitions have been the locus of much disagreement. The issue of delineating a specific postmodern epoch is contentious. There are those who argue that postmodernity does not exist at all; those who position it after modernity, conceptualised as the rise of industrialisation and mass production, who typically nominate start dates from the 1940s to the 1980s; and those who argue the postmodern does not form an epoch but occurs sporadically across a long modernity, beginning in the late eighteenth century with the Age of Enlightenment. There is even less agreement about when postmodernity will come to an end, assuming it has not already ended.

Many of the book-length studies on postmodernism and film come out of Sociology rather than Film Studies. Carl Boggs and Tom Pollard view postmodern cinema as largely reflective of a nihilistic postmodernity, char-acterised by the ending of Enlightenment ideals, the rise of capitalism and a return to a violent Hobbesian state of nature (2003: 1–36, 163–5). They offer thematic analyses of films by key directors such as Quentin Tarantino and Oliver Stone in order to demonstrate that postmodern cinema breaks with humanist values to promulgate a violent, amoral nihilism (2003:

152–74). Norman Denzin (1991) outlines different forms of postmodern phi-losophy and social theory, which set up a variety of key issues and themes that are said to be reflected in specific films. For example he reads *Wall Street* (Oliver Stone, 1987) as failed critique because it references but does not fully embrace a Baudrillardian analysis of capitalism (1991: 88–92).

While the above sociological accounts tend to draw together diverse modes of postmodern theorising, this book focuses on postmodern aes-thetics in order to show how each theorisation of postmodern style sets up a different way of understanding and analysing Hollywood cinema. Although theorists ostensibly agree that the key aesthetic features of post-modern texts include: acute stylisation, a self-conscious concern with 'the very act of showing/telling stories' (Degli-Esposti 1998b: 4), and multiple references to other texts; evaluations of these aesthetic features differ very greatly. Thus, while irony, pastiche and parody are frequently nominated as the key features of postmodern aesthetics, it is important to note that each term is defined and evaluated differently by the specific theoretical system in which it appears. In order to promote awareness of these crucial differences, this book offers an in-depth analysis of three major postmod-ern theorists: Jean Baudrillard, Frederic Jameson and Linda Hutcheon, contextualising their aesthetic models with a view to demonstrating their usefulness and/or limitations for the analysis of Hollywood cinema.

The extensive theoretical disagreement as to the definition and value of postmodern aesthetics does, in part, explain the paucity of postmodern theory within Film Studies. The subject area contains a number of clearly identifiable theoretical groupings, such as psychoanalytic and cognitive film theory; however, 'it is far less easy to identify a distinctive postmodern film theory' (Hill 1998: 103). This is because the diverse forms of postmod-ern aesthetics do not form a coherent body of work that can easily be taken up and applied to another subject area. It is also the case that the key features comprising postmodern style (whether valorised or vilified) clash or overlap with prevailing aesthetic paradigms of the Hollywood film text, thus preventing the postmodern from fitting neatly into the field.

Chapter one maps out the placing of the postmodern within Film Studies, exploring the prevailing aesthetic paradigms, specifically the classical, modernist and post-classical/new Hollywood, and the concep-tual issues arising from the dominance of the first term. This mapping also traces the development of a linear history of style, in which the postmodern occasionally takes the role of a much-disputed final stage. The chapter explores the problems arising from endeavours to construct such a history, finally deploying Jean-François Lyotard to argue that 'postmodern Hollywood' should not be viewed as an epoch following the classical and/ or post-classical; but is more usefully understood as an aesthetic paradigm that emerges at diverse points across the history of Hollywood cinema.

Chapter two begins with an analysis of Friedrich Nietzsche's *Thus Spoke Zarathustra*, drawing on Lyotard's non-linear conception of the postmodern as that which erupts within the modern, to present Nietzsche as the epitome of postmodern theorising. It introduces Nietzsche's vocabulary of nihilism and affirmation, which underpins the analysis of the theories across the book. This chapter addresses two famous nihilistic theorists of the postmodern: Baudrillard and Jameson, tracing the ways their aesthetics impact on the analysis of Hollywood cinema. Jameson's aesthetic model has gained ascendancy in work on the postmodern within Film Studies, and this chapter ends by exploring the problems that this causes through a detailed meta-critical analysis of M. Keith Booker's *Postmodern Hollywood* (2007).

The final chapter explores affirmative models of postmodern aesthetics, beginning with Peter and Will Brooker's Nietzschean model of circling narratives, before addressing Hutcheon's paradoxical postmodernism. These theorists challenge the nihilistic models, providing their own nuanced and positive variants of postmodern aesthetics. Their models are combined with the earlier Lyotardian analysis of postmodern Hollywood. The positive impact of the affirmative models on the analysis of film texts is demonstrated by detailed readings of four films: *Sherlock Junior* (Buster Keaton, 1924), *Bombshell* (Victor Fleming, 1933) and Quentin Tarantino's *Kill Bill: Vol. 1* (2003) and *Kill Bill: Vol. 2* (2004). The in-depth analyses enable the careful tracing of the diverse range of postmodern strategies offered by each film. While it is beyond the scope of this book to provide a definitive non-linear account of postmodern Hollywood, the films chosen span the silent era, the studio era and contemporary Hollywood. They thus provide a taster of the complex textual strategies that become visible by taking up an affirmative postmodern aesthetics of Hollywood cinema.

1 CLASSICAL/POST-CLASSICAL/POSTMODERN

This chapter will set out the ways in which Hollywood has been conceptualised, and the endeavours to map the postmodern within these accounts. It offers a meta-critical analysis of the key concepts governing the theorisation of the development of Hollywood cinema, focusing on the classical, its relation to the modern, the post-classical and the postmodern. This involves looking at historical models of studio-era Hollywood, the Hollywood Renaissance and New Hollywood. My analysis is primarily conceptual – I am interested in the elements that fall outside the frame provided by the classical as well as the theoretical divisions that are kept in play by the characterisation of the different epochs in Hollywood's history.

Within the limited take up of postmodern theory in Film Studies, the dominant trend is to map the postmodern onto existing paradigms and it is usually equated with aspects of the post-classical and new Hollywood. However, what I want to demonstrate across the course of this chapter is that taking up postmodern modes of theorising involves rethinking the nature of particular paradigms – specifically the limits of the classical – and indeed the whole project of historically periodising aesthetic styles. The final section of this chapter will take up Jean-François Lyotard's conception of the temporality of the postmodern in order to escape unconvincing linear models of development or decline, as well as setting up a model of multiple aesthetic forms, including the postmodern.

The Classical

David Bordwell, Janet Staiger and Kristin Thompson aimed to construct a
new theoretical paradigm for analysing Hollywood that would forge strong
links between its aesthetic, industrial and economic aspects. Their aim
is made clear in the preface to *The Classical Hollywood Cinema*: 'to see
Hollywood film making from 1917–60 as a unified mode of film practice
is to argue for *a coherent system* whereby the aesthetic norms and the
mode of film production reinforced one another' (Bordwell *et al.* 1985: xiv;
emphasis added). Thus two things are instantly striking about the classical
paradigm: its breadth of scope (textual to industrial) and its presentation
as a single system. While the dates 1917–60 suggest the new paradigm is
historical, the drive to singularity and universality indicate its basis within
analytic philosophy: 'the idea of a "classical Hollywood cinema" is ultimately a *theoretical construct* and as such it must be judged by criteria of
logical rigour and instrumental value' (1985: xv; emphasis added).

Bordwell's account of the classical utilises traditional aesthetic definitions of the key features of classicism: 'elegance, unity [and] rule-governed
craftsmanship' (1985: 4). The rules that govern Hollywood cinema are said
to be derived from its own discourses, including trade journals, publicity
material and screenwriting manuals. Bordwell consistently privileges narrative: 'telling a story is the basic formal concern' and stresses the unified
nature of the film text: 'unity is a basic attribute of film form' (1985: 3).
Hollywood films are said to be '"realistic" in both an Aristotelian sense
(truth to the probable) and a naturalistic one (truth to historical fact)'
(ibid.). The impression of realism is compounded by editing techniques:
'the Hollywood film strives to conceal its artifice through techniques of
continuity and "invisible" storytelling' (ibid.).

While the classical paradigm does not address the issue of audience reception (see Bordwell *et al.* 1985: xiv), the audience is crucial to
the formulation of two further rules. The film 'should be comprehensible
and unambiguous; and [possess] a fundamental emotional appeal that
transcends class and nation' (Bordwell 1985: 3). The universal model of
spectatorship set out here requires that mainstream cinema be legible to
everyone in the same way. Bordwell argues that this is possible because
any viewer follows the protocols of reading derived from 'the system of
norms operating in the classical style' (1985: 8). Thus the overriding prin-

ciple of narrative causality in the classical is translated by 'the viewer ... into a tacit strategy for spotting the work's unifying features ... sorting the film's stimuli into the most comprehensive pattern' (ibid.). Borrowing terms from Ernst Gombrich, Bordwell argues that the classical film utilises well-known schemata, such as Hollywood film editing, which 'constitute the basis of the viewer's expectations or mental set' (1985: 8). Thus the film's schemata 'elicit particular activities from the viewer', the viewer deciphering the film by trying out and selecting the appropriate elements of their mental set (ibid.).

Bordwell argues that classical narrative takes the form of logical chains of cause and effect that are predominantly character-centred. 'Here ... is the premise of Hollywood story construction: causality, consequence, psychological motivations, the drive toward overcoming obstacles and achieving goals' (1985: 13). Having made 'personal character traits and goals the causes of action' and thus the underlying structure of the narrative (1985: 16), Bordwell is obliged to conceptualise characterisation as fundamentally consistent: 'a character is made a consistent bundle of a few salient traits, which usually depend upon the character's narrative function' (1985: 14). The classical film is said to have two main lines of action: the first is usually heterosexual romance – winning the love of a man or woman is a key goal of many classical protagonists – while the second can take many forms: 'business, spying, sports, politics, crime, show business – any activity ... which can provide a goal for the character' (1985: 16). Importantly, the 'tight binding of the second line of action to the love interest is one of the most unusual qualities of the classical cinema' (1985: 17), giving these films their distinctive unity.

The unity of the classical film text is sustained by Bordwell's analysis of openings and endings. He argues that the classical film offers an opening exposition of events that is 'concentrated and preliminary' (1985: 28). The opening introduces the main protagonists, sets up character goals and often provides key motifs that are utilised across the film. The audience is immediately immersed within the action, the film beginning in *media res*, and thus the 'exposition plunges us into an already-moving flow of cause and effect' (ibid.). Bordwell notes that all the one hundred films in the primary sample had a clearly demarcated ending in the form of an epilogue defined as 'a part of the final scene, or even a complete final scene, that shows the return of a stable narrative state' (1985: 36). Endings frequently rhyme with the opening exposition as well as utilising key motifs and/or running gags from across the film. Importantly, classical narration is said to end only once all the gaps in the narrative have been filled, creating a tightly unified text (1985: 39).

The classical Hollywood film is typically said to show narrative events in temporal order. The exception to this is the complex use of flashbacks from the late 1930s to the 1950s (1985: 41–2). The compression of the story events into the screen time is achieved partly through the use of ellipsis and montage sequences. The 'forward flow of the story action' (1985: 45) is secured by deadlines and appointments, which also integrate with character goals thereby consolidating the cause and effect logic of the narrative. Bordwell comments that 'as a formal principle, the deadline is one of the most characteristic marks of Hollywood dramaturgy' (1985: 46). Another formal principle is the repetition of story information; indeed, he suggests that 'the Hollywood slogan is to state every fact three times' (1985: 31).

Classical Hollywood cinema is said to subordinate space to the construction of narrative. Classical editing techniques are characterised by invisibility, providing a transparent 'plate-glass window' (Bordwell 1985: 50, 59) onto another world. Importantly, Bordwell's construction of classical Hollywood as a series of rule-governed processes is sustained by editing: 'of all Hollywood stylistic practices, continuity editing has been considered a set of firm rules' (1985: 57). Adherence to the 180-degree rule underpins a number of key devices including: shot/reverse-shot patterns, point-of-view editing, eyeline matches and matches on action (1985: 56–8). Moreover such devices act as 'traditional schemata which the classical filmmaker can impose on any subject' (1985: 57) thereby ensuring that the spectator is carefully cued to fill in any gaps. Thus the transparency of the diegetic world is achieved partly through its rule-governed presentation and partly through 'the viewer, [who] having learned distinct perceptual and cognitive activities, meets the film halfway and completes the illusion of seeing an *integral fictional space*' (1985: 59; emphasis added).

Bordwell's vision of the classical can thus be seen to present the Hollywood film text as a tightly unified whole. In addition, his model of a rule-governed stylistic system has a profound impact on Janet Staiger's conceptualisation of Hollywood's production practices. She takes up a circular position, arguing that Hollywood's modes of production are both 'the historical conditions allowing a group style to exist [and] the effect of the group style' (Bordwell *et al*. 1985: 88). She traces the ways in which the institutional discourse – created by advertising, trade papers, professional and labour associations – served to standardise the Hollywood group style and production practices across the industry (1985: 96–108). 'This institutional discourse explains why the production practices of Hollywood have been uniform through the years and provides a background for a group style which [is] also stable through the same period' (1985: 108). Thus the rule-governed stability of the classical model actually acts as both effect and cause: it is the end product of an equally stable production process, and a template for industrial standardisation, uniformity and stability.

Hollywood's production processes are frequently conceptualised as the epitome of capitalist mass production and paralleled with Henry Ford's mass production of automobiles (Bordwell *et al*. 1985: 90). The Fordist-Taylorist assembly-line model of factory production involves a 'detailed division of labour. Here the process of making a product is broken down into discreet segments and each worker is assigned to repeat a constituent element of that process' (1985: 91). Each worker's repetition of one element of the process maximises efficiency, while also ensuring that they have no relation to the end product as a whole. By contrast, Staiger argues that Hollywood's production processes were closer to serial manufacturing 'with craftsmen collectively and serially producing a commodity', an end product to which they all had a relation (1985: 93, 336). She notes that Hollywood's drive towards product differentiation, stressing novelty and innovation in order to lure audiences to the cinema again and again, constitutes a further departure from the Fordist-Taylorist model of the perfect replication of the same product (1985: 109–11).

Staiger's analysis of the institutional discourse of advertising foregrounds the importance of stars, genre and spectacle in the development of Hollywood cinema (Bordwell *et al*. 1985: 95–101). While she follows Bordwell, ultimately subordinating these elements to narrative, their potential to unsettle the paradigm of the classical is suggested at various points across the book. All three elements emerge in Bordwell's analysis of narrative motivation, defined as 'the process by which a narrative justifies its story material and the plot's presentation of that story material' (1985: 19). Motivation is said to take four main forms: compositional, realistic, intertextual and artistic. The example of compositional motivation involves cause and effect: 'a story involving a theft requires a cause for the theft and an object to be stolen' (ibid.). This is presented as the dominant form of narrative motivation, which serves to secure textual coherence. Realistic motivation is based on the principle of verisimilitude. Thus a historical drama will require costumes, props and settings that evoke the period in which the narrative is set.

The third form – intertextual motivation – has the potential to break down Bordwell's model of the hermetically sealed film text because it covers features that are derived from previous texts, such as star persona and generic conventions. Bordwell notes that an audience would expect a film starring Marlene Dietrich to feature her singing a cabaret song at some point. His comment that her number could be 'more or less causally motivated' indicates that the song might challenge the precedence of compositional motivation, temporarily suspending the strict narrative logic of cause and effect (1985: 20). The example is also indicative of a set of viewer expectations established through an aggregate of previous texts rather than the application of particular schemata. Thus informed viewers would not just expect Dietrich to sing but would piece together aspects of her performance, costume and filmic presentation to form a much more complex set of expectations. Distinctive features of Dietrich's star persona, including key elements of androgyny and bisexuality, are actually established via musical numbers, for example her famous appearance in black tie for the 'Quand l'Amour Meurt' number in *Morocco* (Josef von Sternberg, 1930).

The fourth and final type of narrative motivation that Bordwell delineates is artistic motivation in which specific features draw attention to the film's status as a film. He acknowledges that the process of 'calling attention to a work's own artfulness' (1985: 21) appears to challenge his conception of classical cinema as typically transparent and self-effacing. Artistic motivation encompasses all modes of visual spectacle, including displays of 'flagrant technical virtuosity' (ibid.) from lighting design to complex camera movements. It also applies to brief, self-reflexive moments, such as overt references to other films and stars, which draw attention to the film's artifice. For example *My Favorite Brunette* (Elliott Nugent, 1947) in which 'Ronnie Johnson tells Sam McCloud he wants to be a tough detective like Alan Ladd; McCloud is played by Alan Ladd' (ibid.). Bordwell acknowledges that an appreciation of visual virtuosity and aural in-jokes requires a sophisticated viewer: 'To some extent artistic motivation develops connoisseurship in the classical spectator' (1985: 22).

A film may also use artistic motivation 'to call attention to its own particular principles of construction' (ibid.). Bordwell gives the example of the 'You Were Meant For Me' number from *Singin' in the Rain* (Gene Kelly & Stanley Donen, 1952). Don Lockwood (Gene Kelly) carefully places the machinery required to create the right atmosphere for a romantic musical number – coloured lights, mist and a soft summer breeze – before he begins singing to Kathy Selden (Debbie Reynolds), thereby drawing attention to the conventions for staging such numbers. This process of 'baring the device' is said to be common in comedies and musicals, the latter often having narratives which centre on putting on a show (ibid.). While acknowledging the importance of artistic motivation in two major genres, Bordwell asserts that classical cinema 'does not bare its devices repeatedly and systematically' (1985: 23), unlike avant-garde works such as Michael Snow's *La Région Centrale* (1971). As a result, the classical is said to subordinate artistic motivation to compositional motivation.

It is important to note that Bordwell positions the avant-garde method of baring the device as exemplary of pure artistic motivation, setting up the contrast with the classical, which then appears unsustained and inconsistent. In this way reflexivity and the foregrounding of filmic conventions within the classical are positioned as brief, ornamental moments while the fundamental level of meaning is located within the narrative. The privileging of narrative motivation serves to contain the other forms, thereby subordinating a diversity of different aesthetic strategies, specifically intertextuality and reflexivity, in order to maintain the unity of the classical text.

Modernity/Modernism

Miriam Bratu Hansen argues that definitions of the classical within film theory utilise and reinforce long-standing oppositions between classicism and modernism from aesthetics and philosophy (2000: 335–6). E. Ann Kaplan notes the take up of the same oppositions to conceptualise mass culture in her analysis of MTV as a postmodern art form: 'the aesthetic discourse dominant in Western culture from the late nineteenth to the midtwentieth century has polarized the popular/realist commercial text and the "high art" modernist one' (1987: 40). She unpacks the binary oppositions delineating the defining characteristics of classical and modernist/avant-garde texts in a useful table, suggestively entitled 'Polarized filmic categories in recent film theory' (1987: 41). Both theorists draw attention to the ways in which the classical film tends to accrue increasingly negative characteristics when conceptualised as the opposite of the modernist text.

Table 1 Polarized filmic categories in recent film theory

The classical text (Hollywood)	The avant-garde [modernist] text
Realism/narrative	Non-realist anti-narrative
History	Discourse
Complicit ideology	Rupture of dominant ideology

Kaplan runs together the classical text's qualities of realism, narrative and history on the grounds that all three combine to achieve the 'efface-ment of the means of production', covering over the labour of directing and acting as well as technological processes of filming and editing (1987: 40). The Hollywood film creates a 'realistic' diegetic world by offering a narrative that appears to unfold transparently by itself: 'the "story told from nowhere, told by nobody"' (ibid.). This transparency is maintained by the techniques of continuity editing, which are also said to rigidly position the spectator within the narrative flow (ibid.). Moreover, the opposition History/Discourse, here basically synonymous with self-effacing/self-re-flexive, simply erases the categories of narrative motivation that Bordwell was prepared to contemplate, presenting the classical as incapable of baring the device or offering self-reflexive commentary.

Crucially, the absence of such interrogative and self-reflexive tech-niques means that classical texts are seen simply to embody dominant ideology. Bordwell briefly touches on this aspect, noting that the figure of the goal-orientated protagonist is 'a reflection of an ideology of American individualism and enterprise' (1985: 16). However, Kaplan's final tabu-lar opposition draws on older critiques of mass culture, beginning with Theodor Adorno, in which studio-era Hollywood is seen to be absolutely complicit with the values of capitalism. By contrast, the self-reflexive modernist text can offer a 'self-conscious play with dominant forms' that may include 'a critique of mainstream culture', thereby rupturing and subverting dominant ideology (1987: 40–1). The binary of ideological versus progressive plays a crucial role in theories of counter cinema, offered by Peter Wollen, Stephen Heath and Laura Mulvey among others, which have been dubbed 'political modernism' (see Hansen 2000: 337–8). Kaplan's table nicely encapsulates the ways in which aesthetic strategies become synonymous with stark political stances. In three stages the distinction between the classical and the modernist is transformed into an absolute division between ideological complicity and subversion.

Hansen argues that the positioning of Hollywood within the binary of the classical versus the modernist is enormously problematic for two reasons. Firstly, it covers over Hollywood's relation to 'mid-twentieth-century modernity, roughly from the 1920s through the 1950s – the modernity of mass production, mass consumption and mass annihilation' (2000: 332). Secondly, the application of 'stylistic principles modelled on seventeenth-century and eighteenth-century neo-classicism … to a cultural formation that was … perceived as the incarnation of the modern' (2000: 337) is fundamentally anachronistic. Thus the take up of the terminology of the classical ultimately serves to hide Hollywood's relation to a specific historical and cultural context – modernity as experienced in the United States of America.

Hansen suggests that these problems are largely caused by the concept of the classical itself, which 'implies the transcendence of mere historicity', setting up 'a transhistorical [*sic*] ideal, a timeless sense of beauty, proportion, harmony and balance derived from nature' (2000: 338). The shift away from the specificities of cultural context is most obvious in Bordwell's universal model of spectatorship. Narrative and stylistic schemata lead to the development of spectatorial mental sets thereby ensuring that all spectators go about deciphering classical texts in the same way. By contrast, Hansen argues in favour of recognising the culturally diverse nature of Hollywood's global audience. 'If classical Hollywood cinema succeeded as an international … idiom … it did so not because of its presumably universal narrative form but because it meant different things to different people and publics, both at home and abroad' (2000: 341). She notes that key contextual factors such as: programming, censorship, marketing and subtitling, would make for markedly different conditions of reception within different countries, thereby sustaining multiple, culturally diverse readings of the film texts.

Hansen argues that the solution to the problems of the classical model is the repositioning of Hollywood within its historical relation to modernity. She presents Hollywood cinema from the 1920s to the 1950s as 'an aesthetic medium up-to-date with Fordist-Taylorist methods of industrial production and mass consumption, with drastic changes in social, sexual and gender relations, in the material fabric of everyday life' (2000: 337). Thus Hollywood cinema is modern in both its modes of production and consumption as well as having the capacity to reflect on the conditions of modernity. Hansen argues in favour of reconceptualising Hollywood cinema as 'a cultural practice … as an industrially produced, mass based, *vernacular modernism*' (ibid.; emphasis added). In this way, she sets up a distinction between two different modes of reflecting on modernity: modernist works of art and the popular cultural forms of vernacular modernism.

Hansen argues that the cultural forms of vernacular modernism were capable of articulating and embodying many different relations to modernity. Hollywood cinema constituted 'a cultural horizon in which the traumatic effects of modernity were reflected, rejected or disavowed, transmuted or negotiated' (2000: 231–2). Importantly, she suggests that this constitutes a mode of reflexivity that should be distinguished from modernist 'formalist self-reflexivity'. The latter involves the foregrounding of technique for specific effects, typically the distancing of the spectator from the work of art in order to facilitate their developing critical awareness of the work and, indeed, capitalist society and ideology in general. Hollywood cinema is reflexive in that it offers a collective perspective on modernity, thereby acting as 'an aesthetic horizon for the experience of industrial mass society' (2000: 342). Following Siegfried Kracauer, Hansen argues that slapstick films offer this type of reflexive engagement with Fordist-Taylorist industrialisation. Films such as *Modern Times* (Charles Chaplin, 1936) are said to both articulate and disrupt 'the violence of technological regimes, mechanization and clock time' (2000: 343). Her focus on slapstick suggests that a more substantive engagement with the genre of comedy could generate awareness of a multiplicity of reflexive textual practices. Crucially, she challenges modernist definitions, where reflexivity is narrowly aligned with specific forms of social and political critique.

Hansen makes clear that her compelling vision of an ambivalent modernity arises from her position within contemporary postmodern culture; however, she does not address the nature of the transition from modernity to postmodernity (2000: 344). Moreover, her concept of vernacular modernism overlaps with the postmodern on two key issues: the status of mass culture and the delineation of reflexive aesthetic strategies. Finally, Hansen's model draws together the epoch of modernity and the aesthetic strategies of vernacular modernism, presenting a model in which the economic, cultural and aesthetic are all intimately inter-related. This chapter will demonstrate that an effective mapping of postmodern aesthetic strategies requires a fundamental reconsideration of the inter-relations between these diverse aspects.

After the Classical

Determining the end-date of the classical is not at all straightforward. While Bordwell, Staiger and Thompson's original study goes up to 1960, two of the authors have been vehement in their denial of the existence of the post-classical, arguing that contemporary Hollywood demonstrates the longevity of the classical paradigm (see Thompson 1999; Bordwell 2006). Other theorists argue that important changes to economic and industrial conditions in post-war Hollywood serve to usher in an era that has been variously entitled modern, new or post-classical. The key historical changes, such as the end of vertical integration and the demise of censorship, will be outlined here.

The era after the classical also comprises two very differently characterised periods: the 'Hollywood Renaissance', beginning with *Bonnie and Clyde* (Arthur Penn, 1967) and ending in the mid- to late-1970s; and 'New Hollywood', which is synonymous with the rise of the blockbuster, beginning with the advent of *Jaws* (Steven Spielberg, 1975) to the present day. While the precise dates of each historical period are subject to debate, matters are further complicated by a lack of critical consensus concerning terminology. Geoff King notes that some critics use the term 'New Hollywood' for the entire era post-World War II to the present day, others apply it specifically to the decade of the Hollywood Renaissance, while a number use it purely with reference to a cinema dominated by the blockbuster (2002b: 3). This account will treat the Hollywood Renaissance and New Hollywood as two distinct periods, following the historical divisions given at the beginning of the paragraph, in order to set out the characteristic aesthetic features of each period and to trace the ways in which each reprises and reworks key binaries, specifically modernism/classicism, classical/post-classical and modernist/postmodern.

Historians charting the many economic and industrial changes to Hollywood typically assign a key role to the Paramount case of May 1948 in which the Supreme Court ruled that the studio system constituted an illegal monopoly (see King 2002b: 27–9; Krämer 2005: 20). By the 1930s the 'big five' studios – Warner Bros., Loew's Inc., Paramount, Twentieth Century Fox and RKO – all had fully vertically integrated operations, which meant they controlled the production, distribution and exhibition of their films. Tino Balio demonstrates that such dominance resulted in a series of unfair practices, including: '[block] booking, the fixing of admission prices, unfair runs ... discriminatory pricing and purchasing arrangements favoring affiliated theater circuits' (1985: 402). While the big five did not directly control the majority of cinemas country-wide, they owned the majority of the 'movie palaces', major first-run cinemas in big cities, which comprised 70 per cent of the box-office takings for the home market (see King 2002b: 26). The successful prosecution of the big five under antitrust laws against monopoly practices had a number of significant effects.

The mandatory selling off of movie theatres made places of exhibition more independent. They no longer had to purchase blocks of films from one specific studio and no deals could be done between the big five to secure exhibition. Balio notes that the numbers of art-house cinemas across America increased from fewer than a hundred in 1950 to over six hundred by the mid-1960s (1985: 405). These independent cinemas acted as screening outlets for a diversity of products including reissues of Hollywood 'classics', European films and independently-made American films. The studios' loss of their sites of exhibition had a profound effect on film censorship in that it made it impossible to secure the implementation of the Production Code. The Production Code Administration had been set up in 1934, reviewing scripts and previewing completed prints to ensure they met the guidelines of the code. All films had to gain a seal of approval from the PCA before they could be distributed and exhibited (see King 2002b: 29–34). However, the rise of independent art-house cinemas meant films that did not gain a seal could now find sites of exhibition (see King 2002b: 30). Eventually, this inability to enforce the Code led to its replacement with a ratings system in 1968 (see Krämer 2005: 47–9).

The timing of the Paramount decrees was unfortunate for the studios, because it coincided with a very significant decline in audience numbers. Krämer notes that 'average weekly attendance ... plummeted from 82 [million] in 1946 to 73 [million] in 1947' with a further 10 per cent drop each year, falling to 42 million by 1952 (2005: 20). A variety of reasons are given for the decline in numbers: the post-war baby boom, new modes of urban planning that increased suburbanisation and the rise of alternative leisure pursuits, particularly the advent of television during the 1950s (see Balio 1985: 401–2; Bordwell *et al.* 1985: 332; Krämer 2005: 20–1). Importantly, the significant decline of income coupled with the loss of secure sites of exhibition meant that the studios' distinctive 'factory-style system' with 'huge permanent staffs and in-house departments' (King 2002b: 27–8) was now prohibitively expensive.

Historians agree that the period of the late-1940s to the mid-1950s saw the end of the factory-style studio and a rise in independent production (see Balio 1985: 404–5; King 2002b: 28). Janet Staiger charts this shift as a move away from a 'producer unit' system of production in which 'a group of men supervised six to eight films per year ... each producer concentrating on a particular type of film', to a 'package unit' system (Bordwell *et al.* 1985: 320). In the first mode of production, the labour and materials to make a film were offered by a single company: the studio. While in the second, 'a producer organized a film project: he or she secured financing and combined the necessary laborers ... and the means of production' (1985: 330). She notes that agencies could play the role of producer in the package unit system, charting the rising importance of the William Morris Agency and the Music Corporation of America (MCA) (1985: 333). Staiger contends that the shift from the producer unit system to the package unit system did not substantially affect the stability or uniformity of the classical Hollywood production mode (Bordwell *et al.* 1985: 334–5). However, others see the shift as a substantial change (see Schatz 1993; MacDonald 2000; Hall 2002; King 2002b).

The Hollywood Renaissance

Goeff King argues that while key changes to the exhibition, consumption and production of Hollywood films post-1948 'helped to create space for the Hollywood Renaissance', the deciding factor was the financial crisis experienced by the studios in the mid-to-late 1960s (2002b: 34).

Hollywood had two conflicting strategies for dealing with the decline in audience numbers: the targeting of films to specialised, typically adult, audiences, and the creation of lavish roadshow productions that appealed to the broad, family audience (2002b: 34–5). Peter Krämer notes that from 1960 to 1966, 'between one and four of the top five films every year were epics or musicals with roadshow releases' (2005: 40). These big-budget films were lavish productions that required a substantial initial investment, which would then be recuperated during the period of their theatrical run. The crisis came about when the majors 'poured money into a series of musical extravaganzas', such as *Doctor Dolittle* (Richard Fleischer, 1967) and *Star!* (Robert Wise, 1968), which failed at the domestic box office (see King 2002b: 35). At the same time, lower-budget, contemporary productions, such as *Bonnie and Clyde* and *The Graduate* (Mike Nichols, 1967) proved commercially successful, thereby encouraging a trend. The latter cost three million dollars to make and grossed US$105 million at the American and Canadian box offices, coming first in Krämer's table of the ten highest grossing hits of 1967 (2005: 106–7).

Krämer argues that *Bonnie and Clyde* plays a key role in popular and critical conceptions of a new cinema emerging in the mid-to-late 1960s: the Hollywood Renaissance. On 8 December 1967 the cover of *Time* magazine featured a publicity still from the film alongside the caption '"The New Cinema: Violence ... Sex ... Art"'; the article inside the magazine celebrated the film for beginning 'a new style, a new trend', utilising elements of stylistic innovation pioneered by the European New Waves (see Krämer 2005: 1). The film was commercially successful, coming fifth in the top ten box office figures for 1967 after its re-release following critical acclaim in Europe (2005: 106–7). The article in *Time* concluded that '*Bonnie and Clyde* demonstrated ... Hollywood was undergoing a *renaissance*, a period of great artistic achievement based on "new freedom" and widespread experimentation' (2005: 1; emphasis added). It thus presciently outlines some of the defining features of the Hollywood Renaissance as it is conceptualised in later critical writing. It is viewed as a golden era of independent filmmaking, a new form of distinctively American modernism, and an epoch abounding in formally innovative and politically subversive films (see Krämer 1998: 303; 2005: 2).

Part of the novelty of the Hollywood Renaissance was its association with a new generation of film directors. Krämer notes that many of the top hits of 1967–76 were directed by newcomers from the interwar generation. These young directors had not come through the studio system but had instead received their training in television and theatre before starting to make films (2005: 82–4). Indeed both Mike Nichols and Arthur Penn worked on Broadway during the 1960s. This partly accounts for their willingness to directly present subject matter that the Production Code would have regarded as too controversial, such as the adulterous affair in *The Graduate* (see King 2002b: 32). Krämer's delineation of the key directors of this period differs significantly from his earlier summary of standard auteurist accounts of the new generation of directors emerging in the 1960s, which focus on 'the so-called "film school generation" or "movie-brats"' (1998: 303). The close-knit group comprises Martin Scorsese, Brian De Palma, Francis Ford Coppola, John Milius, George Lucas and Steven Spielberg. Critics have argued that the experience of formal education in film created a generation of cinematically and theoretically literate directors who styled themselves as auteurs (see Carroll 1982: 52–5; King 2002b: 88–90).

King's analysis of the textual strategies deployed by films from the Hollywood Renaissance utilises two familiar sets of aesthetic criteria: the modernist and the classical. He offers a detailed analysis of the opening scene of *Bonnie and Clyde*, drawing attention to two jump cuts: the first while Bonnie (Faye Dunaway) turns away from viewing herself in the mirror and the second as she moves to lie, semi-naked, on her bed. Bonnie '[thumps] the bedstead in frustration. She pulls herself up, head framed through the horizontal bars. A sultry pose. The camera lurches awkwardly into a big close-up on her eyes and nose' (2002b: 11–12). The obvious change of focus in the awkward lurch of the camera coupled with the jump cuts shows Penn utilising the techniques of the French New Wave to create an impression of 'restlessness, edginess and … sexual hunger or longing' (2002b: 12). The jump cuts were inspired by Jean-Luc Godard's *À bout de souffle* (1960) and are deployed similarly to create a disorientation and uneasiness that forms the tone of the film (see King 2002b: 12, 36–7, 40).

Tonal disorientation is achieved through spatial dislocation created by eschewing some of the rules of continuity editing, specifically the 180-degree rule and matches on action. King argues that classical editing serves to create the illusion 'of a world that is ordered and comprehensible' (2002b: 39). Thus, disrupting the classical construction of space through the use of jump cuts has ideological significance. However, Penn's departure from the classical construction of space is not sufficient to create a properly modernist text. King's reading charts a course from the modernist to the classical: 'departures from classical conventions can be seen as expressive devices [if they] are "motivated" by matters of character or narrative. As such they remain within the influential definition of classical style given by David Bordwell' (2002b: 41). In this way, King re/reads his own analysis of the opening scene of *Bonnie and Clyde* – the expressive use of disorientating editing techniques means it actually conforms to the classical paradigm. At stake here is a sense in which the binary of the modernist versus the classical contains and confines the aesthetic possibilities of the film text – it must be one or the other. In failing to be sufficiently modernist, *Bonnie and Clyde* becomes classical.

Both King and Krämer are concerned to challenge conceptions of the Hollywood Renaissance as a golden era of politically subversive and/or modernist filmmaking. Krämer's strategy is to show that this description does not apply to most of the top ten films released between 1967 and 1977. In contrast, King demonstrates that Renaissance films do not conform to modernist standards of subversion. While he acknowledges that some Renaissance films are 'openly critical of dominant myths and ideologies', many 'remain within the compass of dominant mythologies' (2002b: 45). Indeed, *Bonnie and Clyde* is seen to update the frontier mythology of the classical western. King notes that *The Conversation* (Francis Ford Coppola, 1974) and *The Parallax View* (Alan J. Pakula, 1974) subvert convention by denying their protagonists 'any possibility of success' or even a heroic death (ibid.). However, the social and political implications of such endings are 'entirely negative. No alternative is offered. Diagnosis is not accompanied by a prescription for change' (ibid.). Thus proper subversion is seen to involve both the deconstruction of the capitalist system and (ideally) the delineation of socio-political alternatives. Once again, the films of the Hollywood Renaissance fail to conform to the standards set by modernist aesthetics.

King's repositioning of Renaissance films as stylistically classical, rather than modernist, expands the historical boundaries of classical aesthetics, moving the paradigm into the 1960s. Interestingly, although a number of the stylised, self-reflexive aesthetic strategies of Renaissance films could be regarded as postmodern, this period does not tend to be conceptualised in this way. In contrast, New Hollywood has been theorised as both the end of classical aesthetics and the beginning of the post-classical. While the post-classical is often collapsed into the postmodern, this account will note the divergence of some key aesthetic strategies.

New Hollywood

Thomas Schatz defines New Hollywood as the era of the blockbuster – suggesting that the label best applies to the post-1975 period, following the success of *Jaws* (1993: 9). Schatz parallels his deployment of the title with Bordwell, Staiger and Thompson's definition of the classical: 'Both terms connote not only specific historical periods, but also characteristic qualities of the movie industry at the time particularly its economic and institutional structure, its mode of production, and its system of narrative conventions' (ibid.). I will address the problematic scope of these definitions later. Sheldon Hall notes that the term 'blockbuster' originates in 1943–44, referring to a bomb big enough to destroy a city block. Its first use with reference to film occurs on 14 November 1951 in a *Variety* review of *Quo Vadis* (Mervyn Le Roy, 1951) where praise for 'plunging horses and necklines (Hall 2008)' sets up immediate associations with action, visual spectacle and excess.

While it is clear that Hollywood has a long history of creating large-scale spectacles, *Jaws* is positioned as exemplary of New Hollywood for a variety of reasons. Firstly, it is an example of a pre-sold property – the film is based on a best-selling novel – thereby ensuring a pre-existing audience for the movie (see King 2002b: 54). Secondly it conforms to the package unit system of production. The deal was brokered by International Creative Management, who represented the book's author, Peter Benchley, and 'the producing team of Richard Zanuck and David Brown [putting] together the movie project with MCA/Universal and *wunderkind* director Steven Spielberg' (Schatz 1993: 17). Finally, and most importantly, *Jaws* both initiates and consolidates major changes in patterns of exhibition and promotion. In the roadshow release model, a limited number of prints toured the country and were exhibited at prestige cinemas. Hall notes that 'publicity costs were typically shared with exhibitors at a local level' and the film built up a reputation through press reviews and word of mouth during the course of the theatrical run (2002: 21). *Jaws* marks a shift to simultaneous release patterns and a significant escalation of promotion. The film was released 'on 464 domestic screens accompanied by a nationwide print and television advertising campaign' (ibid.). The cost of the advertising campaign was US$2.5 million, most of which was spent in the week before the film opened. This campaign of saturation booking and advertising became the new norm, each successive blockbuster aiming to be released on more screens with greater publicity, thus driving up the costs of distribution still further (Hall 2002: 21).

Schatz argues that the shift in patterns of exhibition and promotion had the effect of placing 'increased importance on a film's box office performance in its opening weeks of release' (1993: 19). The front-loading of the audience also ensures a film has an opportunity to recoup production costs before being undermined by any adverse publicity (ibid.). The blockbuster thus overcomes a significant disadvantage of the roadshow model, namely the length of time taken to cover the cost of production. The front-loading of the audience becomes increasingly pronounced with contemporary blockbusters aiming to recoup a large percentage of production costs in their opening weekend. King provides the example of *Batman* (Tim Burton, 1989) which had an estimated production budget of US$30–40 million and grossed US$40 million in its three-day opening weekend (2002b: 56). Profits are also maximised through the creation of multiple platforms of consumption. Schatz notes that '*Jaws* became a veritable sub-industry unto itself via commercial tie-ins and merchandising ploys' (1993: 18).

The accumulation of further profits through marketing tie-ins, as demonstrated by *Jaws*, is part of an ever-expanding trend. The substantial profits for *Star Wars: Episode IV – A New Hope* (George Lucas, 1977), US$510 million by 1980, were augmented by sales of t-shirts and 'intergalactic bubble-gum', the latter grossing US$260,000 in July 1977 alone (see Pirie 1981: 53). King argues that from the 1980s to the early 2000s, the development of ancillary markets became crucial to Hollywood's economic strategy: 'a way of increasing revenues [during] a period in which growth in box-office income was outstripped by escalating production and marketing costs and an increasing share in gross profits was claimed by key creative talent' (2002b: 68–9). Hall notes that throughout the late 1980s and 1990s a blockbuster could 'earn two to three times its domestic gross' (2002: 22) through ancillary markets, such as television and home video.

The shift to viewing the blockbuster as one element of an overall marketing strategy that encompasses a number of inter-related products – the book, the soundtrack, the video/DVD, the game, the bubble-gum and the theme park ride – is brought about by the conglomeratisation of the Hollywood film industry. King notes that the major studios – Warner Bros., Disney, Twentieth Century Fox, Paramount, Universal, Sony Pictures/ Columbia and DreamWorks – 'are located within the landscape of large media corporations' (2002b: 67). This clearly spreads the significant financial risk involved in the production of expensive blockbusters. He traces the way in which the multiple mediums of the *Batman* franchise, including comic books, soundtracks and video releases, demonstrate the potential for the development of ancillary markets through conglomeratisation (see King 2002b: 74–5).

The conglomeratisation of Hollywood can be seen as ultimately homogenising, creating a handful of giant corporations whose tentacles are everywhere. Indeed, King argues that New Hollywood displays two axes of integration: the multiple marketing platforms constituting a mode of horizontal integration while 'old-style vertical integration exists in the combination of production/finance and distribution' (2002b: 71). This has an effect on the range and scope of alternatives available; 'corporate Hollywood sets certain limits on what can be achieved. Space for less obviously commercial or more challenging material is determined to a significant extent by the success of the mainstream blockbuster' (2002b: 83). The takeover of independent distributors/producers by major studios, such as Disney's acquisition of Miramax in 1993, would seem to indicate that even the innovative is now part of the system (ibid.).

In contrast to King's picture of homogenisation, Schatz argues that the defining features of New Hollywood are fragmentation and diversification. He parallels the 'increasingly fragmented entertainment industry' epitomised by 'diversified "multi-media" conglomerates', and its 'equally fragmented' products – the blockbusters with their multiform marketing platforms (1993: 9, 10). Importantly, Schatz's article is formative in the conceptualisation of New Hollywood as post-classical. The 'vertical integration of classical Hollywood, which ensured a closed industrial system and coherent narrative, has given way to "horizontal integration" of the New Hollywood's tightly diversified media conglomerates, which favors texts strategically "open" to multiple readings and multimedia reiteration' (1993: 34). It should be noted that this formulation of the classical significantly reworks Staiger, presenting the studio era alone as the epitome of classical production.

Schatz conceptualises the key aesthetic qualities of the blockbuster as a negation of the classical. The blockbuster does not form an integrated whole and lacks causal narrative structures and effective characterisation. This is because marketing imperatives to create ancillary products have an 'aesthetic corollary': 'films with minimal character complexity ... and by-the-numbers plotting (especially male action pictures) are the most readily reformulated and thus the most likely to be parlayed into a full-blown franchise' (1993: 29). Indeed, the blockbuster is so swamped by ancillary products, it 'scarcely even qualifies as a narrative' (1993: 33). The demise of characterisation is also attributed to the new star system. Key players have simply become 'franchises unto themselves' (1993: 31), making star vehicles that are devoid of character development. Schatz, like many others, presents the demise of narrative as a logical consequence of the rise of spectacle (1993: 12, 23, 32; see also King 2000: 3; King 2002b: 179). The construction of spectacle as destructive typically reduces it to big-budget special effects, which affect the audience in purely visceral and kinetic ways.

King explores the conceptualisation of the blockbuster as 'a virtually non-stop roller-coaster "thrill ride"' (2002b: 185) utilising Fred Pfeil's quantitative analyses. Pfeil's graphs set out three models of the relation between narrative duration (horizontal axis) and spectacular events (vertical axis) in a film. The third graph traces the trajectory of the blockbuster, its line charting 'a series of peaks and troughs resembling [a] roller-coaster structure' (ibid.). King provides his own quantitative analysis of the central section of *Speed* (Jan de Bont, 1994), charting the film after Jack Traven (Keanu Reeves) boards the bomb-laden bus. There are a series of problems: the driver is shot, the bus has to negotiate obstacles, from children crossing to hairpin bends, and, most famously, a gap left in the half-built, new freeway. 'A graphic profile ... would depict a line remaining high in the action-spectacle range and showing ... rapid sequences of sub-peaks' conforming to the roller-coaster pattern (2002b: 190). However, King concludes that the quasi-mathematical calculation of spectacle is problematic, arguing that *Speed* conforms to classical aesthetics in its presentation of a cause and effect narrative chain that is structured around character goals and actions (2002b: 187, 202).

Although Schatz's model of the post-classical has been frequently criticised (see King 2000; King 2002b; Bordwell 2006), it is widely circulated as a summary of the key aesthetic features of the films of New Hollywood and can be set out in the tabular form below.

Classical Hollywood film	Post-classical Hollywood film
Cause and effect narrative	Spectacle
Goal focussed characterisation	Spectacle
Integrated, organic whole	Fragmented/open ended/intertextual
Ordered spectatorial mental sets	Visceral thrills and spills
Ideologically complicit	Ideologically complicit

The post-classical film displays its characteristic fragmentation through textual strategies, particularly intertextual references and generic hybridity (see Schatz 1993: 18, 22, 34). Bordwell's vision of the logical, rule-governed processes of classical spectatorship can be pitted against the visceral thrill-rides of the post-classical spectator. At the same time, the post-classical open-ended text does sustain the construction of multiple readings, suggesting the possibility of more complex modes of spectatorship. Both types of text are ideologically complicit for different reasons. The self-effacing narrative techniques of the classical secure its construction of a hermetically-sealed world thereby ensuring it fails to challenge dominant ideology. While the foregrounding of spectacle in the blockbuster might have reflexive possibilities, these are circumvented by its status as one product in a raft of commodities, and thus it epitomises and endorses capitalist ideology.

While the table sets out the key oppositions attributed to classical/ post-classical film texts, it is clear from Schatz's analysis that one pair of aesthetic terms, integration versus fragmentation, play a privileged role in welding the aesthetic to the economic and industrial elements. The aesthetic term thus functions as a crucial metaphor, holding the disparate elements together. Both Schatz and King analyse the rise of conglomeratisation, but each characterises the process differently – as diversification and ever-tighter integration respectively. This demonstrates that it would be equally viable to view the industrial conditions of conglomeratisation as integration, thereby destroying the industrial aspect of a paradigm of the post-classical based on fragmentation. At stake here is the recognition that the metaphor of fragmentation is under considerable strain in the production of the post-classical paradigm.

King's deployment of classical aesthetics to analyse films of the Hollywood Renaissance and New Hollywood positions Bordwell's account of classical style alongside historical accounts of modes of production that are seen as a break with the classical, such as the rise of independent production during the 1960s and the conglomeratisation of the 1980s. King thus fundamentally undermines the parallel between 'aesthetic norms and the mode of film production' that is the basis of the classical paradigm (Bordwell *et al.* 1985: xiv). If the products of the conglomeratised New Hollywood display classical aesthetic strategies, they cannot be causally related to classical modes of production. Moreover, the reverse postulation that the creation of classical narratives is a major aim of multi-media conglomerates seems even less plausible. The economic organisation of New Hollywood would suggest that Hollywood's imperatives are mainly commercial (see King 2002b: 180–1).

Post-classical/Postmodern

Film theorists have taken up different aspects of the post-classical and related them to the postmodern. Linda Williams focuses on the shift in modes of spectatorship, from mental sets to visceral thrills, arguing that they demarcate a key transition from the classical to the postmodern. This shift in viewing techniques is said to be initiated by *Psycho* (Alfred Hitchcock, 1960). The unprecedented murder of the protagonist, Marion Crane (Janet Leigh), halfway through the film, effectively deprives the audience of their locus of identification and their normal modes of deciphering narrative. Instead, spectators are left 'to anticipate "Mother's" next attack and to register the rhythms of its anticipation, shock, and release' (2000: 356). Thus *Psycho* begins the process of recreating spectatorship as a series of visceral thrills and spills, encouraging a '"roller-coaster" sensibility' (ibid.). This postmodern sensibility is further integrated with other aspects of the post-classical, in that it shows a dwindling of spectatorial 'concern for coherent characters or motives' (ibid.).

The problem with Williams' equation of the post-classical and the postmodern is that it constitutes an unusual use of the terminology of the postmodern. Postmodern theory presents the world as a text, one that is constantly constructed and reconstructed through competing discourses, and thus is frequently criticised for its failure to conceptualise the bodily and the visceral except as a series of signs. As a result, the model of the bodily spectator that Williams wishes to promote would not seem to be best served by the label 'postmodern'. Other endeavours to inter-relate the post-classical and the postmodern centre on the aesthetic strategies of fragmentation and intertextuality. I will explore one of these versions in detail, Roberta Garrett's analysis of New Hollywood's relation to the postmodern, which draws heavily on Nöel Carroll's influential article on allusion in Hollywood cinema from 1982.

Carroll's article focuses on films made from the 1960s to the early 1980s, thereby conjoining the periods of the Hollywood Renaissance and New Hollywood to form a single era entitled 'new Hollywood' (1982: 74–5). He argues that films from this era display a distinctive aesthetic feature – they contain unprecedented quantities of allusion (1982: 51). Carroll defines allusion as an 'umbrella term' that includes 'quotations, the memorialization of past genres, the reworking of past genres, *homages*, and the recreation of "classic" scenes, shots, plot motifs, lines of dialogue, themes, gestures, and so forth from film history' (1982: 52). The explosion of allusion in Hollywood cinema is the result of a general enthusiasm for film history that seized America in the 1960s and early 1970s (1982: 54). This was caused by the widespread dissemination of archive Hollywood films through independent cinemas and the medium of television.

This widespread enthusiasm for film history coupled with education at film school resulted in a new generation of cinematically literate directors who style themselves as auteurs (see Carroll 1982: 54–5). Importantly, Carroll initially argues that allusion both draws on and sustains auteurism. For example, some 1970s' directors are said to refer to Howard Hawks' films in order to 'assert their possession of a Hawksian world view, a cluster of themes and expressive qualities that has been … expounded in the critical literature' (1982: 53). Thus an allusion to Hawks both recreates elements from one of his films' diegetic worlds and references critical writing on the distinctive perspective of Hawks the auteur (1982: 55). In turn, the use of allusion reconstructs the new directors themselves as auteurs in that they 'unequivocally identify *their point of view* on the material at hand' (1982: 53; emphasis added). Importantly, in this initial definition, allusion is not equated with 'plagiarism or uninspired derivativeness', it is a vital 'part of the expressive design of the new films' (1982: 52).

Such allusive texts could only be fully appreciated by a cinematically literate spectator and Carroll develops a two-tier model of the audience: the naïve 'adolescent clientele' positioned below the 'inveterate film gnostics' who have the cultural capital to play the 'game of allusion' (1982: 55–6). Both types of spectator are at variance with the thrill seeker of the post-classical model. Carroll also conceptualises the film text as divided, comprising 'the genre film pure and simple, and ... the art film in the genre film' (1982: 56). Successful blockbusters, such as *Star Wars* and *Raiders of the Lost Ark* (Steven Spielberg, 1981), please both tiers of the audience by offering a 'loving evocation' of past genres, imitating and exaggerating the B-movie cliffhanger (1982: 62). The generic allusions in *Raiders of the Lost Ark* have expressive qualities, producing a nostalgic 'wistfulness and yearning' (ibid.). At the same time, the lavish quality of the reconstructions repackage 'the potboiler prototypes so that they are finally as breathtaking as we want to remember them' (ibid.). Carroll notes that such celebratory allusionism is neither ironic nor defamiliarising, and concludes: 'the aesthetic risk of *Raiders* is that the line between a genre memorialization and tawdry genre rerun ... may become all but invisible' (1982: 64).

Carroll argues that the widespread practice of allusion ultimately changes 'the nature of Hollywood symbol systems', charting a move-ment away from a natural integration of form and content to a system of shorthand: 'organic expression for a Hawks was translated into an icono-graphic code by a Walter Hill or a John Carpenter' (1982: 55). The result is the formation of a specific type of allusion that works via 'iconic reference rather than ... expressive implication' (1982: 69). The shift away from the natural and expressive to 'style-as-symbol' comes to be constructed as a form of decline. This is evident from Carroll's later comments in which allu-sion is repositioned as 'part of a more general recent tendency to *strident stylization*' (1982: 78; emphasis added) evident in the films of the new Hollywood.

Carroll's article constructs two narratives of decline: the shift from natural expression to an iconographic code and the transition from expressive allusion to mere affectation. Carroll's first, positive form of expressive allusionism is related to a distinctive utopian social project: 'a desire to establish a new community, with film history supplying its legends, myths and vocabulary' (1982: 79). However, this utopianism is located firmly in the 1960s and later forms of allusion are in danger of deteriorating into 'mere affectation [and] nostalgia' (1982: 80). In this second form, allusion is the practice of the despised *metteur-en-scène* rather than the auteur, 'presenting the artist in terms of ultra-competence rather than genius, as technically brilliant rather than profound, as a manipulator rather than an innovator' (1982: 80, fn. 16). In this second formulation, allusion is equated with derivativeness.

While Carroll's article has been taken up to chart the relation between new Hollywood and the postmodern (see Dika 2003; Garrett 2007), he only touches on postmodern aesthetics in a single footnote. He distinguishes between Hollywood allusionism, which is expressive, and postmodern intertextuality, which 'refers to artifacts of cultural history for reflexive purposes, urging us to view the products of media as media' (1982: 70, fn. 14). The binary of expressive versus reflexive is problematic given Carroll's own charting of the decline of expressive allusion and the rise of 'strident stylisation' across the era of new Hollywood. Moreover, the characterisation of the reflexive qualities of the postmodern – the foregrounding of the medium itself – sounds more akin to modernist aesthetic strategies.

Roberta Garrett takes up Carroll's work in order to chart the development of new Hollywood and its relation to the postmodern. She argues that new Hollywood promotes two textual strategies that intersect with those of an emerging 'popular postmodernist cinema aesthetic' (2007: 28): allusions to classical texts and generic hybridity. Garrett sets up a three-stage model of allusion that constitutes a key map of the development of postmodern cinema within Film Studies (2007: 33, 42–44). The first two stages roughly correspond to the periodising explored in this chapter: the Hollywood Renaissance followed by the rise of the blockbuster.

Garrett's model sets out an overall trajectory of decline, following Carroll's narrative of the degeneration of allusion. There is a 'first wave of auteurist allusionism – in which new Hollywood directors sought to pay homage to the best of classical and European art cinema' (2007: 42). This is followed by 'the blockbuster celebration of older action and adventure forms', such as *Star Wars* and *Raiders of the Lost Ark* (ibid.). The third stage of 'postmodernist self-reflexivity is marked by its range of "lowbrow" subcultural, popular references and specific appeal to … viewers whose formative years were steeped in an unprecedented exposure to classic and contemporary cultural forms' (ibid.). Thus the key aesthetic feature of postmodern film is the sheer quantity and diversity of intertextual references. Postmodern allusionism is often viewed as undiscriminating, evident from its characterisation as 'cinematic stew' or a magpie collection or ragbag of references (Brooker and Brooker 1997a: 90; Booker 2007: 48).

The director who epitomises the third stage is, of course, Quentin Tarantino. Garrett contrasts his eclectic range of lowbrow references – famously gained from working in a video store – with the cine-literate backgrounds of the movie brats. The third form of allusion is the most debased because it constitutes a recycling of all past forms, regardless of their cultural status: 'it reflects the … film industry's tendency to plunder, cannibalise and repackage older forms as "classic" largely on the basis of their value as signifiers of the past as opposed to their continued relevance or cultural worth' (2007: 42–3). The shift in terminology, from auteurist allusionism to mere repackaging, encapsulates both the narrative of decline and the impact of conglomeratisation. Defined as 'repackaging', the aesthetic strategy of allusion is simply synonymous with the marketing strategies of the multi-media conglomerates. Like Schatz's use of fragmentation, the term 'repackaging' operates on a metaphorical level, welding together the aesthetic and industrial elements.

The problem with Garrett's attempt to interweave the decline of allusion and the rise of conglomeratisation is the weakness in the delineation of the second stage. The allusionism of the second stage is characterised as unproblematically celebratory, yet this period marks the beginning of conglomeratisation. Indeed, the strategies of the blockbuster – simultaneous release patterns, saturation booking and the escalation of advertising – both constitute and initiate new extremes of capitalist economics. It is thus not at all clear how the allusionism of films of the second stage escapes the debasement of the allusionism displayed by films from the third stage. Indeed, Carroll's ambivalence towards tawdry genre reruns suggests they do not (see 1982: 64). If the major difference between films from the second and third stages is simply the sheer quantity and diversity of references, then the transition is purely aesthetic and has no straightforward economic and industrial correlates.

The problems arising from Schatz's definition of the post-classical and Garrett's delineation of the postmodern foreground a fundamental issue: namely the sheer impossibility of delineating a single model that could weld together the economic, industrial and aesthetic elements successfully. Schatz's explicit endeavour to create another version of the classical paradigm thus highlights the untenable scope of the original. Moreover, the presentation of post-classical and postmodern aesthetic strategies as the products of specific historical epochs is undercut by the recognition that only a proportion of the films made during the designated epoch will exhibit such strategies (see Schatz 1993: 35; Garrett 2007: 22). Garrett, like King, contributes to the perpetuation of classical aesthetics, arguing that numerous products of new Hollywood conform to this model (2007: 22).

The argument that new Hollywood films exhibit features of classical aesthetics has the logical corollary of drastically loosening the historical dimension originally indicated by the terminology of 'the classical'. Indeed, the expansion of the classical era of 1917–1960 from 1917 up to the present day would seem to mark the end of its usefulness as a means of historical classification. Bordwell and Thompson's demonstrations of the longevity of classical aesthetics focus on editing and narrative construction rather than the means of production, thereby shifting the terms of the original paradigm. Importantly, Bordwell's defence involves a shift in the formulation of classical aesthetics from a rule-governed process to the rules underpinning the process. No longer (partly) presented as one of a series of aesthetic styles, such as classical versus modernist, Hollywood's classical aesthetic becomes the rules of narrative and style, forming 'the default framework for international cinematic expression' (2006: 12).

Bordwell's later presentation of the classical as a foundational framework is achieved through parallels with the Italian Renaissance. The classical premises of narrative and/or style established in the studio era are compared with 'the principles of perspective in visual art' (2006: 12). In contrast, the aesthetics of the post-classical – displayed by films from directors working after the demise of the studio system – constitute a specific aesthetic style. The post-classical directors' efforts 'to respond to the powerful legacy of studio-era cinema' (2006: 16) are compared with post-Renaissance painters' attempts to delineate their own styles in the shadow of their illustrious predecessors. Thus Bordwell suggests the strident stylisation of new Hollywood can be paralleled with Mannerism in Italian painting of the sixteenth century (2006: 188). Both exhibit the following key aesthetic features: overt stylisation, self-consciousness and a celebration of artifice (2006: 188–9). Importantly, the foundational principles of the classical remain unchanged by the transition. Indeed, just as the rules of perspective underpin Mannerism, the principles of the classical set up the possibility of a post-classical style.

This shift from aesthetic features to underlying rules can be seen in the analysis of classical narrative. Bordwell's discussion of narrative experimentation in new Hollywood is grounded by a key question: 'How could innovations be made comprehensible and pleasurable to a wide audience?' (2006: 73). The question alters the status of classical narrative; it no longer functions as one type of tightly integrated story structure but rather as a set of rules of storytelling that ensure a narrative is comprehensible. The shift is made possible through a slippage in the precise purview of 'the rules'. For example, cause and effect is first presented as 'a premise of Hollywood story construction' (1985: 13). Its purview is expanded to the audience when it is reintroduced as a chief principle of 'intelligible exposition': the means through which a narrative can be understood by the viewer (2006: 93). As a result, films as diverse as *Groundhog Day* (Harold Ramis, 1993) and *Memento* (Christopher Nolan, 2000) are repositioned as classical insofar as the viewer is able to construct a fabula that conforms to causal logic (see Bordwell 2006: 78–80, 91–3).

The repositioning of cause and effect as a principle of intelligibility simply foregrounds the highly tenuous nature of its link to the classical. The logical structure of causality and its usefulness for everyday reasoning has a long history within Western philosophy, beginning with Aristotle, thus preceding the model of classical Hollywood cinema by about two millennia. A viewer's use of causal reasoning to understand narrative does not therefore constitute evidence of the dominance of the classical. Moreover, the reworking of the classical extends the aesthetic aspects of the first paradigm. Classical narration is initially defined by its forward flowing temporality (1985: 45), a feature that would seem to be undermined by the inclusion of *Memento*. If most new Hollywood films are basically classical, it is not because they all obey the same fundamental rules, but rather that the aesthetic parameters of the model are being continually reworked, becoming so elastic that the designation of 'classical' is applicable to everything. Thus the apparent dominance of *the* classical paradigm is attained through the constant reinterpretation of what constitutes the classical, thereby setting up a series of inter-related paradigms under a single name.

Bordwell keeps the term 'post-classical' in play in order to rebut the category by demonstrating that the products of new Hollywood are still classical. The eschewal of the post-classical is, unsurprisingly, accompanied by a rejection of the postmodern. Bordwell aims to 'get past generalizations about blockbusters and postmodern fragmentation' by showing that such texts adhere 'to very old canons' (2006: 35). This involves finding historical antecedents for the blockbuster in the 'chases, stunts, fights and explosions' (2006: 108) featured in early classical films, such as *Our Hospitality* (John G. Blystone & Buster Keaton, 1923) . However, the delineation of precedents for the blockbuster's celebration of spectacle merely repositions the blockbuster as a continuation of trends begun in the historical era of the classical. It does not address the crucial issue, namely that the narrative-dominated theoretical model of classical aesthetics makes it impossible to discern and map the development of such aesthetic trends. Incorporating the blockbuster within the paradigm of classical aesthetics forecloses any mapping of the different roles played by spectacle in different genres of film. This is the point at which the expanded paradigm of the classical ceases to be of instrumental value, its all-encompassing nature prevents the charting of different types of aesthetics.

The Meanings of 'Post-'

Bordwell, Staiger and Thompson present their first paradigm of the classical as a model of scientific reasoning that is based on unbiased sampling (1985: 10). However, their view of the history of Hollywood cinema as the rise of a single paradigm, including production contexts, technological innovation and aesthetics, creates an overarching narrative that betrays the legacy of Enlightenment theorising. One of Jean-François Lyotard's key examples of a grand narrative is Marxist theory. It offers an overarching telos of progress, the eventual overthrow of capitalism by the workers themselves, alongside a key foundational term, economics, which acts as the site of truth. Within the classical paradigm, the overriding metaphors of unity and integration serve to weld together the disparate industrial and aesthetic elements. The rhetoric of norms, rules and standards also functions to secure the singularity of the paradigm, acting as a bridge between Bordwell's aesthetics and Staiger's account of standardisation in production. Moreover, Bordwell's conceptualisation of classical aesthetics positions narrative as the key foundational term – it operates as the privileged site of textual meaning. Bordwell's later paralleling of studio-era Hollywood and the Italian Renaissance creates a pinnacle of attainment within the narrative of the classical, thereby outlining a trajectory of rise and fall.

Theorists who argue for the end of the classical set up competing but similarly overarching narratives: Schatz's charting of the post-classical, Carroll's delineation of the demise of allusion in new Hollywood, and Garrett's account of the advent of the postmodern all offer teleological narratives of inexorable decline. The problem in all these cases is the attempt to construct the new era as a clearly delineated epoch. In these conceptualisations of the post-classical and the postmodern, the term 'post' 'has the sense of a simple succession, a diachronic sequence of periods in which each one is clearly identifiable' (Lyotard 1992: 90). Each new epoch is also characterised as a complete break: 'a conversion: a new direction from the previous one' (ibid.). Lyotard argues 'this idea of a linear chronology is itself perfectly "modern". It is at once part of Christianity, Cartesianism and Jacobinism: since we are inaugurating something completely new, the hands of the clock should be put back to zero' (ibid.). For Lyotard, the modernist conception of a complete break is particularly suspicious: 'this rupture is in fact a way of forgetting or repressing the past … repeating it and not surpassing it' (ibid.).

Within Film Studies, narratives of conversion, such as Schatz's model of the post-classical, have been swiftly followed by narratives of continuity – Bordwell's defence of the classical. However, combatting narratives of conversion through the assertion of continuity also involves the suppression of the past. The key aesthetic features inadequately conceptualised within the original classical paradigm – intertextuality, spectacle and self-reflexivity – are repressed once again by the reassertion of the dominance of narrative. Importantly, the failure of every attempt to contain the aesthetic strategies of Hollywood cinema within specific historical periods, from the classical to the postmodern, shows that the division of aesthetic styles into discrete epochs simply cannot be done. The logical corollary of the widely held claim that classical aesthetics can be found in films outside the classical period (see Schatz 1993: 35; Garrett 2007: 22) is to accept that post-classical and postmodern aesthetic strategies can be found in texts made during the classical period.

Lyotard's critique of the use of the term 'post' to indicate successive periods, leads him to argue that postmodern aesthetics cannot be equated with or confined to a postmodern era. For Lyotard, the postmodern continually erupts within the modern, destroying any construction of a linear timeline. Postmodern art differs from modern art in its relation to the sublime. Postmodern art is 'that which searches for new presentations ... in order to impart a stronger sense of the unpresentable' (1984b: 81). Lyotard continues his analysis of the non-linear temporality of postmodern art forms by charting their relation to the formation of rules. 'A postmodern artist or writer is in the position of a philosopher: the text he writes, the work he produces are not in principle governed by pre-established rules, and they cannot be judged ... by applying familiar categories to the text or to the work. Those rules and categories are what the work of art is itself looking for' (ibid.). Thus the incommensurability of the creation of postmodern texts and the later critical/theoretical understanding of their aesthetic strategies are part of the temporal paradox of the postmodern. Such postmodern texts help to bring new rules into existence: 'The artist and the writer [work] without rules in order to formulate the rules of what will have been done' (ibid.).

I want to draw on Lyotard's conception of the temporality of postmodern aesthetics as a means of solving the problems arising from unsuccessful attempts to periodise aesthetics within Film Studies. Utilising Lyotard enables us to begin to chart the ways in which texts from different epochs in Hollywood history utilise postmodern allusive and intertextual strategies. The acknowledgement that Hollywood's aesthetic strategies do not conform to neat periodisations does not imply that all historical periodisation is impossible. Charting local changes to specific conditions is essential to constructing the economic, industrial and technological histories of Hollywood cinema. Within this century-long period, historical demarcation points, such as the studio era or the decade of the Hollywood Renaissance, can be helpful.

The binary of classical versus post-classical aesthetics dominates much of the writing on new Hollywood. One way out is to argue that the post-classical is a misnomer and such films are really classical. Others, like Richard de Cordova, have focused on the star system to argue that Hollywood films are inherently intertextual, thereby offering another overarching model (1991: 25–6). In contrast, I want to argue that the Hollywood film text can take a range of aesthetic forms, indicated by adding postmodern Hollywood film to the previous tabulation of classical and post-classical aesthetics to create a triptych. The delineation of three options effectively undermines the apparently all-encompassing scope of the binary oppositions set up by the first two columns. Crucially, the triptych form also visually repositions the classical as one particular aesthetic paradigm among many – it does not have the status of foundational principles from which all the other styles are derived. This repositioning is crucial to maintaining the terminology of the classical as a viable designation of an aesthetic style. The term only has meaning when compared and contrasted with other styles, which, in turn, set clear limits to its applicability and scope. Finally, the table is not a definitive summary but a useful starting point for the investigation of different models of postmodern aesthetics that follows in the next two chapters.

Classical Hollywood film	Post-classical Hollywood film	Postmodern Hollywood film
Cause and effect narrative	Spectacle, loose episodic narrative	Self-conscious narration
Goal focussed characterisation	Spectacle, lack of character development	Self-reflexive spectacle Abbreviated, artificial characterisation
Integrated, organic whole	Fragmented/open ended/ intertextual	Allusive, intertextual, parody, pastiche
Ordered spectatorial Mental sets	Visceral thrills and spills	Pleasure of deciphering Humour/laughter
Ideologically complicit	Ideologically complicit	Complicit or not?

Postmodern texts foreground the techniques of storytelling, offering forms of self-conscious narration, as well as using allusion to reference previous stories (Degli-Esposti 1998: 4). Such texts draw attention to their means of construction, foregrounding their own artifice and use of convention. Characterisation is typically stylised, drawing attention to its conventional status through the use of stock types or particular performance styles. Character construction can also take an abbreviated, short-hand form given that part of the work may be done by intertextual references. Importantly, as will become evident, postmodern allusion is not necessarily synonymous with fragmentation. The intertextual references may well contain elements that can be incorporated into the spectator's construction of a diegetic world. The drawing together of intertextual cues needs to be differentiated from Bordwell's model for reading a classical film text. The latter involves the reconstruction of narrative that centres on the goals of key protagonists, which instigate tightly integrated causal chains of events. Thus the classical does not have the monopoly on all forms of textual integration – it constitutes one specific construction of narrative integration.

I have retained the category of the post-classical because it has been widely utilised as an aesthetic model in the popular press. I have added further explanatory detail to the first two rows, positioning spectacle alongside 'loose, episodic narrative' rather than simply equating it with a lack of narrative. Williams' analysis of the postmodern spectator can therefore be repositioned as an account of the post-classical spectator, which is appropriate given its use of four of the five categories. The final column breaks down the traditional binary of mind versus body set up by the logical classical spectator and visceral post-classical viewer. The pleasures of deciphering and laughter are both conceptual and emotional. Laughter is positioned as a key spectatorial response given the dominance of parody in much theoretical writing on postmodern art forms. The issue of whether or not postmodern films are ideologically complicit will be explored across the following chapters. Where postmodern reflexivity is understood to be a failed attempt to perform proper modernist reflexivity, postmodern films are assumed to be ideologically complicit. Broadening the category of reflexivity – as Hansen does – thus involves rethinking the necessarily complicitous status of the different types of Hollywood aesthetic. Taking Lyotard's conception of the temporality of the postmodern seriously enables us to move backwards and forwards noting key instances of postmodern aesthetics in Hollywood without constructing an overarching narrative of development or demise.

Importantly, as I have demonstrated, postmodern aesthetics cannot simply be grafted onto current historical and/or aesthetic paradigms for mapping Hollywood. It does not fit neatly into the parameters of the post-classical, nor can it be added on as a final stage in the development of new Hollywood. The inclusion of postmodern aesthetics within Film Studies does not simply leave the field as it was. Thus this chapter has demonstrated what is at stake in all postmodern theorising – it is disconcerting and challenging – taking it up involves rethinking the conceptual categories through which Hollywood's aesthetics have previously been mapped. The next two chapters will examine which versions of postmodern aesthetics are most useful for thinking about Hollywood.

2 NIHILISTIC POSTMODERNISMS

This chapter will explore the work of key theorists who offer nihilistic constructions of postmodernity and postmodern aesthetics: Jean Baudrillard and Frederic Jameson.* This will involve outlining their overall position before focusing on their respective constructions of postmodern aesthetics and their relation to Hollywood cinema. I will demonstrate that Jameson's work has been the most influential in the conception of postmodern Hollywood, which will involve analysing the book-length adaptation of his position by M. Keith Booker. My overall argument will show that the take up of Jameson's conception of postmodern aesthetics in relation to Hollywood cinema seriously circumscribes the aesthetic possibilities of postmodern Hollywood film.

I want to begin this chapter by introducing the work of Friedrich Nietzsche because he holds an undisputed place as a key predecessor to postmodern theory. The first section of Lawrence Cahoone's anthology, *From Modernism to Postmodernism* (1996), offers single extracts from Descartes, Hegel and Kant while including four extracts from Nietzsche's works. Following the temporal structures of Lyotard's model, Nietzsche's work can be reappraised as an eruption of postmodern theorising within the modern. While Lyotard finds elements of the postmodern sublime in both Kant and Burke,

---

* Baudrillard is positioned before Jameson in this chapter because *Simulacra and Simulation* was first published in French in 1981, and *Simulations* followed in 1983.

he does not locate it in Nietzsche. However, reviewing Nietzsche's work as that of a philosopher in search of rules that come into being as he writes is helpful for thinking about the ways in which his writing and writing style encapsulate many of the key tenets of postmodern theorising. Moreover, Nietzsche sets up a distinction between nihilistic and affirmative models of theorising that will be utilised across chapters two and three.

Friedrich Nietzsche

As can be seen from its title, *Thus Spoke Zarathustra* is a parody of the Bible in which Nietzsche's prophet protagonist, Zarathustra, announces the death of God and the birth of the overman. Zarathustra is characterised as a teacher; like John the Baptist he comes to pave the way, rather than constituting a new Messiah. 'Behold I teach you the overman. The overman is the meaning of the earth. Let your will say: the overman *shall be* the meaning of the earth! I beseech you my brothers, remain faithful to the earth, and do not believe those who speak to you of otherworldly hopes' (Nietzsche 1982: 125). In this quote, the declamatory rhetoric of the prophet is used to undermine the Christian hope of an afterlife or Paradise. Indeed such hopes are denounced as poisonous for they teach people to devalue and neglect earthly life, the material world and their bodily presence within it.

In contrast to the blueprint of the good life and good soul set out in the New Testament, Zarathustra repeatedly characterises the overman as a process and not a final state: 'What is great in man is that he is a bridge and not an end: what can be loved in man is that he is an *overture* and a *going under*' (1982: 127). The process of going under is the opposite of the movement of reaching Heavenwards typical of Christianity. Moreover the rhythmic balance of the over – the overture as new beginning – and the going under is typical of Nietzsche's prose style, undermining any sense of attaining a fixed state. The imagery of the bridge is later expanded to form 'the rainbow and bridges of the overman' (1982: 163). Here the image of the rainbow reworks the bridge to form an arcing structure whose endpoint, according to folk-lore, can never be found.

The journey of becoming that constitutes the overman is fundamentally linked to the question of value, requiring man to break away from all imposed, external values – particularly those of Christianity – and to begin generating his own values. It should be noted that only a male subject can pursue the project of becoming an overman (1982: 178–9). Zarathustra offers the narrative of a three-stage metamorphosis that man must undergo in order to become the creator of his own values: becoming a camel, a lion, and finally a child (1982: 137–40). The camel speeds into the desert, the biblical setting for trials of spiritual endurance. Once in the depths of the desert, the camel becomes a lion and 'seeks out his last master ... and his last god', the great dragon '"Thou shalt"' (1982: 138). The name of the dragon clearly recalls the famous formulation of the Ten Commandments in Exodus, thus 'values, thousands of years old, shine on [its] scales' (1982: 139). Becoming a lion is crucial to summoning up the strength to prey on the dragon, which involves disillusion and destruction: 'He once loved "thou shalt" as most sacred: now he must find illusion and caprice even in the most sacred, that freedom from his love may become his prey: the lion is needed for such prey' (ibid.). Preying on the dragon requires 'a sacred "No" even to duty' (ibid.). Importantly, the strength of the lion is not enough to create new values. The transition from the second to the third stage constitutes a crucial shift from negation to affirmation. Thus the destructive nihilism of the lion gives way to the creative, positive power of the child, who is characterised as: 'a new beginning, a game, a self-propelled wheel, a first movement, a sacred "Yes"' (ibid.).

In the fourth part of *Thus Spoke Zarathustra* the titular protagonist meets a multiplicity of diverse characters, including two Kings, the last Pope, the Ugliest Man, the Shadow and the Magician. Each is caught within their own crisis of values caused by the death of God and each, in turn, has a different understanding of Zarathustra's project: the heralding of the overman. The two Kings take up Zarathustra's metaphorical search for 'the higher man', another variant of the one who goes over. However, they look for a man 'who is higher than we, though we are kings ... For the highest man shall also be the highest lord on earth' (1982: 358). The Kings' interpretation of Zarathustra's project echoes the misrepresentation of Christ's mission presented by the second temptation. The Devil takes Christ up to the top of a high mountain, showing him 'all the kingdoms of the world' and offers him the chance to rule over them (Luke 4: 5–8). In the same way, the Kings interpret the higher man as a leader of nations, and thus fail to recognise that the overman is something they should aspire to become. The last Pope, now retired, offers a different reading. Describing himself as 'a festival of pious memories and divine services' he seeks out Zarathustra, 'the most pious of all those who do not believe in God', in the hope of finding a new saint to venerate (1982: 371–2).

Both the Pope and the Ugliest Man (so-called because he is the murderer of God) offer stories of the death of God that focus on pity. The Pope argues that God was 'harsh and vengeful' in his youth but eventually became 'a shaky old grandmother ... weary of the world ... and one day he choked on his all-too-great pity' (1982: 373). The Ugliest Man argues that he had to kill God because 'his eyes ... saw everything; he saw man's depths ... This most curious, overobtrusive, overpitying one had to die' (1982: 378). The predicament of the Ugliest Man tempts Zarathustra to display an emotion that he preaches against, namely pity for others, which briefly overwhelms the prophet during the initial stages of their encounter. Importantly, the proliferation of different stories of the death of God foregrounds inconsistencies in His characterisation across the Bible. Thus Nietzsche's imitation of the Bible's multiple story form draws attention to the impossibility of finding one true meaning – the true character of God – thereby fundamentally undermining the status of the Bible as the Truth.

The two characters who embody key aspects of postmodern theorising are the Shadow and the Magician. Both characters accept and closely follow aspects of Zarathustra's teachings, constituting its most dangerous subversion. The Magician offers this reaction to the loss of Truth in the last stanza of his song of melancholy:

> Burned by one truth,
> And thirsty:
> Do you remember still, remember, hot heart,
> How you thirsted?
> *That I be banished*
> *From all truth,*
> *Only fool!*
> *Only poet!*
> (1982: 412)

Having once thirsted for the salvation proffered by the one Truth, one Way and one Life, the Magician now seeks banishment from all truth. The Shadow also constructs the death of God as the end of all truth but additionally addresses the issue of value. The Shadow takes on the role of Zarathustra's darker double, caught at the second stage of the three metamorphoses, utterly disillusioned and destructive. 'With you I broke whatever my heart revered; I overthrew all boundary stones and images ... over every crime I have passed once' (1982: 386). The loss of truth underpins the Shadow's new freedom to be immoral/criminal: 'Nothing is true, all is permitted' (ibid.). Both characters are trapped within a nihilistic logic of negation, unable to move beyond what they have lost and create alternative value systems of their own.

The Magician's song of melancholy utilises key tropes from Zarathustra's preaching. The second stanza reworks the image of the predatory lion from the second metamorphosis to present Zarathustra himself as a predator:

An animal, cunning, preying, prowling,
That must lie,
That must knowingly, willingly lie:
Lusting for prey,
Colorfully masked,
A mask for itself,
Prey for itself—
(1982: 410)

Having brought about the demise of the Truth, the predator is elided with lies. The imagery of the colourful mask suggests theatricality and illusion; however, as there is no truth to be found lurking behind the mask, the predator becomes 'mask for itself' (ibid.). As the division between face and mask collapses, so too does the binary of predator/prey and thus the predator becomes: 'Prey for itself' (ibid.).

The last part of the second stanza compares the colourful mask of the predator with the poet's use of figurative language:

That, the one who is free from truth?†
No! Only fool! Only poet!

---

† I am very grateful to Rachel Jones for providing the new translation of this line of the poem. Kaufmann's version reads '*This*, the suitor of Truth?'

Only speaking colorfully,
Only screaming colorfully out of fools' masks,
Climbing around on mendacious word bridges,
On colorful rainbows,
Between false heavens
And false earths,
Roaming, hovering—
Only fool! *Only* poet!
(Ibid.)

Like the predator that has become the mask, language itself becomes mere rhetoric – colourful lies. The references to 'mendacious word bridges' and 'colorful rainbows' rework Zarathustra's descriptions of the overman, fore-grounding their status as metaphors while simultaneously equating figurative language and lies. Thus the images no longer function as a description of the overman, they are merely words. At a reflexive level the poem itself screams colourfully using invective and repetition: '*Only* fool! *Only* poet!'

The Shadow also presents the loss of God as fundamentally changing the nature of language. The loss of faith in words empties out their significance, thereby depriving them of depth. For the Magician all language becomes colourful rhetoric, while for the Shadow language becomes exteriorised, material surfaces. Speaking to Zarathustra, the Shadow notes: 'With you I unlearned faith in words and values and great names. When the devil sheds his skin, does not his name fall off too? For that too is skin. The devil himself is perhaps – skin' (1982: 386). Importantly, the Shadow equates the loss of depth of meaning with the loss of all objectively rooted values – specifically the fundamental distinction between good and evil. The Shadow himself is wasting away: 'I have already sat on every surface; like weary dust, I have gone to sleep on mirrors and windowpanes: everything takes away from me' (1982: 384). For both characters there is nothing left but surfaces: masks, skin and dust.

The many characters that encounter Zarathustra, offering variant versions of his teaching, actively demonstrate one of Nietzsche's most famous theoretical moves: the rejection of objective truth in favour of perspectivalism. Thus the end of objective truth, played out by the narratives of the death of God, opens up the possibility of a variety of different perspectives that are embodied by different characters. Each perspective can be seen as a lens that sets up a particular field of vision, in this case the different views of Zarathustra's preaching. Each is intrinsically linked to the values of the viewer and thus clashes of perspectives are also clashes between incommensurate value systems. Perspectives are constantly constructed by individual subjects; however, it is also possible for a perspective to be shared. Indeed, significant congruence between perspectives is indicative of shared values – such as the nihilism espoused by both the Magician and the Shadow. Importantly, the perspectival is not synonymous with the subjective. Being subjective is typically understood as the opposite of being objective and a subjective viewpoint is that of a single individual. The end of objective truth thus marks the end of the category of the subjective as well.

The end of objectivity also means that the many versions of Zarathustra's teachings cannot be judged to be straightforwardly true or false. Importantly, the criteria for judging between perspectives are pragmatic – they are to be judged by their effects. For Zarathustra, perspectives can be more or less healthy – they affect the bodily subjects that articulate them. Harmful perspectives reject the material, often in favour of the transcendental, while those that are healthy celebrate materiality and the body. Thus the Shadow's self-annihilating nihilism constitutes a degenerate perspective. His dilemma leads to the following response from Zarathustra: 'You have lost your goal; alas, how will you digest and jest over this loss?' (1982: 387). The linking of the body and laughter – the enjoyment and exuberance of the child's 'Yes' – is a key feature of affirmative perspectives. The move towards digesting and jesting over the loss of God is played out by many of the key characters in the celebratory ass festival at the end of the book.

In Zarathustra's absence, all his followers who have congregated at his cave conjoin to hold a service, 'kneeling like children and little old women and adoring [an] ass' (1982: 424). The Ugliest Man offers up 'a pious, strange litany' to glorify the animal (ibid.). On returning to the cave, Zarathustra's immediate reaction is to admonish his guests for falling back into their old ways. His first interpretation of the bizarre scene is supported by the comments of the last Pope: 'Better to adore God in this form than in no form at all' (1982: 426). However, the Ugliest Man presents the entire scene in a different light, underscoring the ridiculousness of his own litany by commenting: 'Whoever would kill most thoroughly, *laughs*' (1982: 427).

The ass festival offers an extreme parody of the worship of an inappropriate object, recalling the golden calf that Aaron made from the earrings of women and children (Exodus 32: 2–4). The golden calf is itself an example of the perversion of 'proper' worship. Aaron creates the idol before constructing 'an altar before it' in accordance with detailed instructions set out earlier in Exodus. The ass festival is thus a parody of a distortion of a ritual, its extreme form suggesting that all ritual might be nothing other than distortion and nothing more than laughable.

Significantly, Zarathustra's response to the 'roguish answers' offered by the Ugliest Man is to change his interpretation of the scene (1982: 428). In this way, one of the final sections of the book shows its prophet-protagonist shifting his perspective, making it impossible to simply equate all his speeches with the truth. Having regarded the ass festival as an unfortunate symptom of relapse, Zarathustra shifts to viewing it as comic and thus indispensable to recovery. 'Do not forget this night and this ass festival, you higher men. This you invented when you were with me and I take that for a good sign: such things are invented only by convalescents' (1982: 428–9). His followers' enjoyment and expression of 'a little brave nonsense' displays a childish 'prankishness', which can be seen as a momentary instantiation of the third stage of metamorphosis, and thus part of the process of becoming that constitutes the overman (1982: 428).

At a reflexive level the comments made by the Ugliest Man: 'Not by wrath does one kill, but by laughter' (1982: 427), draw attention to a key strategy of *Thus Spoke Zarathustra*. The book itself is a biblical parody that is designed to bring about the death of God and the undermining of Christian values. At the same time the book offers its own mode of theorising as fiction, setting up new concepts and narratives – such as the overman – while reflexively drawing attention to the fictional and rhetorical nature of these constructs. The use of key aesthetic strategies of reflexivity and parody, and the presentation of theory as fiction, ensure *Thus Spoke Zarathustra* can be viewed as a paradigm of postmodern theorising. Zarathustra's distinction between degenerate and affirmative perspectives can also be applied to theory. Those trapped within the degenerate logic of negation are simply the antithesis of the systems and values that they reject; while theories that affirm life create and express new fictional concepts that are linked to diverse systems of value. Both of these categories are useful for thinking through different modalities of postmodern theorising.

Jean Baudrillard

Baudrillard's famous essay 'The Precession of Simulacra' begins with a quote attributed to Ecclesiastes: 'The simulacrum is never that which conceals the truth – it is the truth which conceals that there is none. The simulacrum is true' (1983: 1). The quote itself cannot be found in the book of Ecclesiastes, leading some commentators to argue that it is an example of simulation, albeit an unconvincing one: 'no one even remotely familiar with Ecclesiastes would be taken in by it' (Hanley 2003: 48). The falsely attributed quotation parodies the declamatory tone typically associated with Old Testament prophets, while also offering a perfectly balanced epigram, both key stylistic features of Nietzsche's writing. The epigram undoes two sets of oppositions: the simulacrum as false copy is typically opposed to the true original; while the truth is typically opposed to concealing lies. In Baudrillard's formulation it is the very concept of the truth that acts as a mode of concealment, covering over its own absence or impossibility. The declamatory opening of this essay is important, because Baudrillard is repeatedly characterised as the 'high priest' of the postmodern rather than a philosopher or cultural theorist (see Gane 1993: 21). Thus the pronouncement: 'The simulacrum is true' marks the moment at which Baudrillard reinvents himself as Zarathustra, becoming the prophet-protagonist of his own postmodern writings.

Baudrillard sets up his own narratives of the death of God in *Simulations*, presenting the collapse of Christianity as concomitant with the rise of the image. In its first form the image 'is the reflection of a basic reality' (1983: 11). This is the premise of representation in which an image is a copy of the real. It is also the model for the creation of mankind who is made in the image of God (Genesis 1: 27). In the second stage the image 'masks and perverts a basic reality' (1983: 11). This conception of the destructive power of the image can be traced back to the Ten Commandments with the explicit prohibition against 'any graven image' (Exodus 20: 4). Baudrillard provides another parody of a biblical quotation: '"I forbad any simulacrum in the temples because the divinity that breathes life into nature cannot be represented"' (1983: 7). In this second stage the image is an 'evil appearance' opposed to the truth and reality presented by God.

The crucial shift is introduced at the third stage when the image 'masks the *absence* of a basic reality' (1983: 11). Here iconolaters, worshippers of idols/images, are celebrated for having 'the most modern and adventurous minds, since underneath the idea of the apparition of God in the mirror of images, they already enacted his death and his disappearance' (1983: 9). However, the worship of God in the form of images also enables the iconolaters to avoid having to face up to his absence, thereby showing their knowledge that 'it is dangerous to unmask images, since they dissimulate the fact that there is nothing behind them' (ibid.). In this quote the image as mask suggests concealment, the mask implies a face; however, its unmasking would reveal that it conceals nothing. Baudrillard links this third stage to magic: the image 'plays at being an appearance – it is of the order of sorcery' (1983: 12).

In the fourth stage the image 'bears no relation to any reality whatever: it is its own pure simulacrum' (1983: 11). This stage is represented by the iconoclasts whose desire to destroy all images arises not from the image's distortion of reality – as in the second stage – but rather from 'despair [at] the idea that the images concealed nothing at all' (1983: 8). This, in turn, affects their status as God's creation: 'in fact they were not images, such as the original model would have made them, but actually perfect simulacra forever radiant with their own fascination' (1983: 8–9). In the fourth stage, the absence of truth and reality underpinning the third stage is explicitly acknowledged. Importantly, the final stage constitutes 'the order of ... simulation', marking the beginning of the postmodern, an era in which there is no longer any reality – only the hyperreal (1983: 12).

Baudrillard argues that there is a crucial shift from stages one and two, which are both characterised by 'a theology of truth and secrecy', to stages three and four, in which there can be no distinctions between true/ false, reality/artifice. His characterisation of stage three as the order of sorcery recalls Nietzsche's Magician, whose song of Melancholy utilises the figure of the masked predator, becoming 'mask for itself', in order to demonstrate the collapse of the distinction between the face and the mask and the impossibility of finding the face (1982: 410). For Baudrillard, the iconography of the mask retains the potential to suggest the face beneath, even where that face/truth has disappeared. He thus utilises the terminology of simulation in order to set up a contemporary figure for an artificiality/fakeness that has no relation to an original/truth.

Stages one to four of the image are frequently presented as successive, a series of phases leading up to a postmodernity located in Western culture in the late twentieth century. However, the introduction of the concept of the simulacrum via (admittedly fake) biblical quotations does also suggest that the phases constitute different ways of theorising the role of the image, which have been available for two millennia. Baudrillard repeatedly combines biblical language with contemporary examples thereby confusing linear temporality. For example, stage three of the image is exemplified by the iconolaters and Disneyland. The latter constitutes an overly fake, childish world thereby presenting its surrounding environs as a real, adult world; 'when in fact all of Los Angeles and the America surrounding it are no longer real, but of the order of the hyperreal and of simulation' (1983: 25). While Baudrillard's apocalyptic characterisation of postmodernity as the end of truth and reality fuels its status as a new era; his denunciation of the 'new' degenerate epoch is part of a familiar cycle – the prophet returns to denounce the state of the world once again.

Like Nietzsche, Baudrillard links the existence of God with depth of meaning, rewriting Blaise Pascal's famous wager. Pascal argued that it was better to wager that God did exist and live one's life accordingly because the potential reward of eternal life in Paradise outweighed all the other, less positive, alternatives. Baudrillard's version links God to the issue of representation and meaning: 'All of Western faith and good faith was engaged in this wager on representation: that a sign could refer to the depth of meaning, that a sign could exchange for meaning and that something could guarantee this exchange – God, of course' (1983: 10). As Alpha and Omega, the beginning and the end, God is the point where multiple interpretations settle into the recognition of the one Truth, thereby underpinning the whole system of meaning.

Thus, for Baudrillard, the absence of any divine anchoring point of language is the moment at which interpretations of any given text or event proliferate uncontrollably. A bombing in Italy can be equally viably regarded as 'the work of leftist extremists, or of extreme right-wing provocation, or staged by centrists to bring every terrorist extreme into disrepute [or] a police-inspired scenario in order to appeal to public security' (1983: 31). 'All of this is equally true' for postmodernity is characterised by a dizzying 'vertigo of interpretation' that cannot be stopped (ibid.). This constitutes a move beyond Nietzsche's perspectivism, which sets up the possibility of a plurality of diverse and shared perspectives that are rooted in willed value systems. For Baudrillard, the infinite proliferation of interpretation 'results in an improvisation of meaning, of nonsense, or of several simultaneous senses which cancel each other out' (1983: 75, fn. 4).

The multiple interpretations of the bombing in Italy utilise a series of oppositions: right versus left, terrorists versus the state police, in order to render them all equivalent. Thus Baudrillard's analysis of language is also an attack on structuralist linguistics in which binary opposition is regarded as one of the primary building blocks for creating meaning. For example, understanding the meaning of the sign 'happy' requires an understanding of its opposite, 'sad'. Structuralist readings involve the elucidation of the fundamental oppositions that underpin any given text. In such readings, oppositions act as foundational structures wherein meaning is stabilised. By contrast, Baudrillard's interpretations of the bombing show the 'conjunction of the system and its extreme alternative' in which oppositional terms such as: right/left, terrorists/state police, become 'circularised'; this is extended into a metaphor for language itself: 'All the [oppositional] referentials intermingle their discourses in a circular, Moebian [*sic*] compulsion' (1983: 35). The movement of the circle and the Mobius strip is a folding over that overflows the stroke separating oppositions, undoing the difference between the terms. In this way, Baudrillard's metaphors of flowing circularity and circulation undermine the structuralist attempt to stabilise meaning around key oppositions.

Baudrillard replays these two key moves: undoing opposition and introducing ceaseless circulation, in his analysis of the rise of capital. Recalling the third phase of the image, capital is defined as 'a *sorcery* of the social relation' (1983: 29, emphasis added) that undermines the very concept of society. Capital, like the image, practices sorcery insofar as it undermines key oppositions: 'it was capital which … shattered every ideal distinction between true and false, good and evil, in order to establish a radical law of equivalence and exchange' (1983: 43). The shift to an economy of exchange is related to the demise of use value. Marx argues that a commodity's utility is determined by its physical properties; for example, wool is a material that keeps us warm. In contrast, exchange value is 'characterised by total abstraction from use value' (1867). Commodities are no longer considered as material objects with specific qualities, but purely in terms of the quantities of other commodities for which they can be exchanged: 'a quarter of wheat is exchanged for x blacking, y silk or z gold' (ibid.). Thus exchange value is built on a sense of the interchangability of all goods thereby setting up an economic model of circulation.

Baudrillard expands upon Marx, arguing that the overproduction of goods in the late twentieth century leads to a further level of divorcement from the materiality of the commodity. Goods are purchased because consumers wish to buy into specific lifestyles established through advertising. Thus the advertising image marks the final obliteration of the commodity's use value, and the reality/materiality of the object itself. Indeed, this is the moment whereby the rise of capitalism ushers in the hyperreal. Just as the loss of divine anchorage in language leads to the proliferation of interpretation, the loss of the anchorage of use value results in the unchecked proliferation of goods and advertisements. For Baudrillard, the excessive nature of late twentieth century capitalism produces an extreme form of the economics of exchange, reworking it as continual, relentless circulation.

Importantly, Baudrillard abandons the Marxist polemic concerning the exploitation of the workers within capitalism. Firstly, the Marxist concept of ideology that covers over 'the "objective" process of exploitation' (1983: 48) belongs to the second stage of the image and we are in the fourth stage, the order of simulacra and the hyperreal, where there are no truths hiding beneath the image. Secondly, the key motif of circulation is further utilised to map the breakdown of the distinction between exploiter and exploited. Thus, for Baudrillard, 'power is something that circulates and whose source can no longer be located, a cycle in which the positions of dominator and the dominated interchange in an endless reversion which is also the end of power in its classical definition' (1983: 77, fn. 7). In this analysis of the circulation of power and capital, both are dehumanised, divorced from any conceptions of ownership or responsibility. The motifs of circulation and floatation sustain a sense of a system generating itself and operating within its own terms: 'Power floats, like money, like language, like theory' (Baudrillard 1994: 24).

Baudrillard's analysis of the excessive nature of postmodern capitalism reaches its zenith in his travelogue *America*. The country is said to offer a vision of liberation as an 'orgy of indifference, disconnection, exhibition and circulation' (1988: 96). The motif of circulation is conjoined with spectacle, advertising and fashion to sustain a sense of a voiding of depth: 'Politics frees itself in the spectacle, in the all-out advertising effect ... mores, customs, the body and language free themselves in the ever-quickening round of fashion' (ibid.). The end of the classical conception of power is, of course, the end of party politics and of viable political intervention. These aspects of Baudrillard's nihilistic conception of postmodernity are challenged by all the theorists in the next chapter. Baudrillard's move to the surface echoes Nietzsche. While the Shadow and the Magician conceptualise language as a pure surface, as skin, dust and masks, Baudrillard views postmodernity and postmodern aesthetics as an 'extravaganza of undifferentiated surfaces' (1988: 125).

For Baudrillard, the subject itself has also been reconstructed as pure surface. The postmodern subject is compared to technological innovations, such as the hologram and the clone, and contrasted with older, psychoanalytic formulations that draw on the figure of the double. The double 'like the soul, the shadow, the mirror image, haunts the subject' (1994: 95). Nietzsche's character of the Shadow acts as the darker double of Zarathustra, reworking his teachings in negative and destructive ways. The double is both the antithesis of the subject and a figure of its unconscious mind – the hidden depths within the rational, conscious, well-behaved exterior. Baudrillard sets up a complex metaphor, comparing the hologram to a double extracted from the body by 'luminous surgery' (1994: 106). 'The double that hid in the depths of you (of your body, or your unconscious?) and whose secret form fed precisely your imaginary, on the condition of remaining secret, is extracted by laser, is ... materialized before you, just as it is possible for you to pass through and beyond it' (1994: 107). The materialisation of the double in three-dimensional laser form – as the hologram – marks the end of unknown inner depths and thus the very structure of the unconscious mind. The postmodern subject like the hologram is pure visual surface. In the final, most exuberant image of the chapter, the hologram 'literally jumps over its shadow, and plunges into transparency to lose itself there' (1994: 109).

Baudrillard's writing on cinema draws on many of the images associated with the postmodern subject. Cinema is paradoxically presented as exemplary of both the pre-modern and the postmodern (see Constable 2009b). The first characterisation of cinema is the most positive. 'The cinema is an image. That is to say not only a screen and a visual form, but a myth [retaining] something of the double, of the phantasm, of the dream, etc' (1994: 51). Here the cinema keeps the tropes associated with inner depths of the subject in play. It is also strongly linked to the imagination and the imaginary: 'pure fascination, the magic appeal of the image.

There is still a strong make-believe quality about the cinema' (Charbonnier 1993: 30). The 'quality of myth' that characterises cinema is not the same as Greek mythology (1993: 31). The mythic is associated with particular forms of narrative presented by both history and the novel: 'the possibility of an "objective" enchainment of events and causes and the possibility of a narrative enchainment of discourse' (Baudrillard 1994: 47). Importantly, the shift from pre-modern to postmodern cinema is characterised as a destruction of the mythic, the fantasmatic and the magical. 'It is this *fabulous* character, the mythical energy of an event or of a narrative, that today seems increasingly lost' (ibid.).

The shift from the pre-modern to the postmodern is thus presented as a narrative of the decline and fall of cinema: 'its trajectory from the most fantastic or mythical to the realistic and the hyperrealistic' (1994: 46). For Baudrillard, postmodern cinema is epitomised by 'remakes' a term that encompasses films such as *The Last Picture Show* (Peter Bogdanovich, 1971) and *Chinatown* (Roman Polanski, 1974). Both display an 'implacable fidelity ... to the restitution of an absolute simulacrum of the past' (1994: 47) insofar as they offer perfect reconstructions of a past that is already constructed through photographic and cinematic images. The remake thus constitutes a move into the hyperreal because it actually builds image upon image. In attempting to achieve 'an absolute correspondence with the real, cinema also approaches an absolute correspondence with itself – and this is not contradictory: it is the very definition of the hyperreal' (ibid.). All endeavours to achieve perfect reconstructions of the past or of the real simply result in the recycling of images that are said to constitute true history/reality. Thus the search for the real results in a further proliferation of images, thereby ushering in the hyperreal. Locked into an utterly circular process, cinema 'plagiarizes and copies itself, recopies itself, remakes its classics, retroactives its original myths, remakes the silent film more perfectly than the original, etc' (ibid.).

Baudrillard's analysis of the decline and fall of cinema focuses on its effects – the many ways in which the remake unwittingly serves to usher in the hyperreal. At the same time postmodern remakes are seen to possess distinctive and familiar aesthetic qualities. While couched in the damning terms of plagiarism, such films are characterised as resolutely intertextual, referencing the history of cinema from the silent era onwards. The remake offers a perfected, flawless version of the past images that it references.

Thus, for Baudrillard, *The Last Picture Show* is 'perfect retro, purged, pure, the hyperrealist restitution of 1950s cinema', because it has removed 'the psychological, moral and sentimental blotches of films of that era' (1994: 45). The alliterative overemphasis on 'purged, pure' perfection draws attention to the depths the surface lacks – psychology, ethics and emotion. In place of the depths provided by characterisation, audience engagement or even meaning, cinema displays 'technical perfection' (1994: 46). In a later interview, Baudrillard links the absence of depth (in the forms of magic and myth) to postmodern reflexivity: 'cinema has become a spectacular demonstration of what one can do with the cinema, with pictures, etc' (Gane 1993: 23). Baudrillard's focus on the intertextual and the interlinking of the spectacular and the reflexive overlaps with elements of the definition of postmodern film aesthetics set out in chapter one. However, the characterisation of such aesthetic strategies as plagiaristic, utterly superficial and void of meaning is clearly problematic.

Baudrillard connects the remake's project of perfecting the image and the reflexivity of postmodern films to the rise of new cinematic technologies. Postmodern films are seen as mechanical/mathematical demonstrations of the capabilities of the new technologies. Thus, *Chinatown*, a remake of 1940s film noir, is described as 'the detective movie renamed by laser' (1994: 46). The pursuit of technical perfection is problematic. Becoming 'hyper-realist, technically sophisticated, effective' postmodern cinema fails 'to incorporate any element of make-believe' or imagination (Charbonnier 1993: 30). In a typical rhetorical move, Baudrillard reverses the linear model of technological development as progress: 'as if the cinema were basically *regressing towards infinity*, towards … a formal, empty perfection' (ibid.; emphasis added).

Baudrillard's somewhat abstract conception of the remake as a process of perfecting the image requires further illustration. It is best exemplified by so-called shot-for-shot remakes in which the hypertext acknowledges its reliance on the anterior hypotext. Indeed, Universal's publicity campaign for Gus Van Sant's *Psycho* (1998) asserted that the director had 'followed Joseph Stefano's dialogue line by line, and John Russell's camera work shot by shot' (see Constable 2009c: 23). The opening of Alfred Hitchcock's *Psycho* (1960) begins with 'a dissolve from the vertical lines of the credit design to the high-rise buildings of an urban skyline credited as "Phoenix, Arizona"' (2009c: 27). This is followed by three long shots of the bright, white cityscape, also linked by dissolves, which culminate in a long shot of a hotel, taken at a high angle, and the camera zooms in on an open window. The subsequent medium shot positions the camera almost directly in front of the window and it tracks forward, the sliding movement into the darkened room suggesting an intrusion into a private space. Indeed the hotel room is the secret rendezvous for a pair of illicit lovers, Marion and Sam. The opening utilises lighting – brightness versus darkness and two different camera movements – zoom and track – to set up key oppositions between public and private, external façade and inner depth. These oppositions play a crucial role in the presentation of the film's monster, Norman Bates.

Van Sant's *Psycho* opens with a circling shot of the city taken from a helicopter. Interestingly, this can be seen as an attempt to be more authentic than Hitchcock's film – the helicopter shot was part of the original shooting script but proved to be too costly to make (see Constable 2009c: 24). The airborne camera travels across the cityscape towards the hotel and the aerial shot is digitally edited to create the effect of a seamless camera movement through the open window, across the sunny bedroom towards the lovers on their bed. It is easy to read the use of digital editing techniques as an attempt to 'perfect' the image, the apparently seamless shot acting as a spectacular demonstration of the new technologies available in the 1990s. Thematically the opening shot obliterates the oppositions set up by Hitchcock. Thus, in this example, the process of perfecting the image is also the annihilation of the concepts of private space and inner depth. For Baudrillard, such a voiding of depth is also a voiding of meaning, affect and imagination, leaving the film solely capable of demonstrating its own technical virtuosity. However, the opening shot need not be read as devoid of meaning, its destruction of oppositions sets up a key theme of the remake, which, as I have argued elsewhere, 'explicitly plays out and plays with the loss of the secret and the impossibility of hidden depths' (2009c: 26).

The application of Baudrillard's model of postmodern film aesthetics to a specific remake such as Van Sant's *Psycho* foregrounds the limitations of this model for Film Studies. It sets up a frame through which such films can *only* be seen as nihilistic demonstrations of the end of aesthetics. It is therefore unsurprising that Baudrillard's writing on film has not been taken up extensively in Film Studies. Indeed, the brief flurry of writing on Baudrillard and *The Matrix Trilogy* (Larry and Andy Wachowski, 1999, 2003) does not address the ways the trilogy might exemplify a Baudrillardian aesthetic. One of the few exceptions is William Merrin's analysis of the trilogy's use of CGI, which he reads as an example of the 'hyperclean, hyperliteral perfection of the digital image' (2005: 122) that destroys the imaginary, imaginative, magical qualities of the cinematic image. Overall, most of the writing focuses on the trilogy's presentation of Baudrillard's postmodern philosophical position – particularly his work on the hyperreal and simulation (see Constable 2009a).

Any consideration of Baudrillard's contribution to postmodern aesthetics has to assess the impact of his distinctive writing style. His narratives of destruction are charged with a gleeful energy that belies their overt nihilism, creating disjunctions between tone and content, and rendering them profoundly ambiguous. While Nietzsche's parody of the Bible in *Thus Spoke Zarathustra* functions as a clear rejection of Christianity, Baudrillard's use of fake quotation evokes Ecclesiastes by offering a parody of a parody of the declamatory style associated with the Old Testament, a series of moves away from any 'original'. Jason de Boer argues this is characteristic of Baudrillard's theory-fiction, in which the theory functions 'as fiction or literature that repeatedly draws attention to its own lack of grounding' (2005: 4). The loss of grounding is also demonstrated by the quantity of incompatible narratives of decline across *Simulacra and Simulation*, the unstoppable movement of proliferation characteristic of postmodernity is thus played out reflexively across the text as a whole. The personification of an array of theoretical concepts, including the hologram, shadow and clone, constructs them as fictional characters thereby drawing attention to their status as theory-fiction. The foregrounding of the fictional through the use of textual strategies such as disjunctive tonality, parody and reflexivity make Baudrillard's writing a paradigm of postmodern theorising.

Frederic Jameson

Baudrillard and Jameson have very different ways of writing theory: the former is a postmodern theorist; while the latter is a theorist of the postmodern. While Jameson's introduction to *Postmodernism, or, The Cultural Logic of Late Capitalism* (1991) utilises elements of the fictional in his presentation of the postmodern as a radical break away from the modern, he does not present his theorising *as* a mode of fiction. Thus the acknowledgment that he has 'pretended to believe that the postmodern is as unusual as it thinks it is', is not an admission of the groundlessness of such theorising, but rather constitutes 'an inaugural narrative act that grounds the perception and interpretation of events to be narrated' (1991: xiii). In this way, the references to fiction and pretence are used to establish a singular moment of grounding that anchors the writing to follow, conferring on it the status of a theoretical hypothesis rather than fiction.

As a Marxist theorist, Jameson's conception of postmodernity is anchored in the economic, specifically the development of late capitalism. Following Ernest Mandel, he distinguishes 'three fundamental moments in capitalism' (1991: 35) The first is market capitalism where goods are created for national markets, the second, monopoly capitalism, which is characterised by world markets organised around nation states, and the third is multinational or late capitalism where national boundaries are undermined by the creation of global markets (see Jameson 1983: 112–15). For Jameson, late capitalism constitutes 'the purest form of capital yet to have emerged, a prodigious expansion of capital into hitherto uncommodified areas' (1991: 36). Importantly, Mandel's tripartite economic model is the basis for Jameson's own 'cultural periodization', which interlinks the economic, the social and the cultural (ibid.). The three phases of market, monopoly and multinational capitalism are thus said to constitute three eras, each dominated by a different cultural/aesthetic form: 'realism, modernism, and postmodernism', respectively (ibid.).

While Jameson argues that late capitalism underpins postmodernism, he briefly notes that his strict paralleling of the economic and the cultural appears to collapse the two terms into each other in an 'eclipse of the distinction between base and superstructure' (1991: xxi). The collapse of base into superstructure is too extreme for Jameson who immediately counters, restoring the distinction by arguing that 'the third stage of capitalism ... generates its superstructures with a new kind of dynamic' (1991: xxi). Importantly, the threatened collapse is an example of the undermining of the spatial logic of depth and surface, which Jameson presents as characteristic of postmodern theory. Postmodern theory is said to follow poststructuralism in attacking 'the depth model' of truth and meaning set up by traditional hermeneutics (1991: 12). Jameson traces the annihilation of traditionally oppositional terms that rely on the distinction between depth and surface such as: inside/outside, essence/appearance and latent/manifest. Like Baudrillard, he notes that the loss of the construction of truth as depth entirely undermines traditional Marxist conceptions of the false surface, specifically ideology and false consciousness. While both theorists characterise the postmodern in terms of the pure surface, Jameson's assertion that 'depth is replaced by surface, or by multiple surfaces' (1991: 12) lacks the playful exuberance of Baudrillard's 'extravaganza of undifferentiated surfaces' (1988: 125).

Both Baudrillard and Jameson argue that the postmodern shift to the surface has a significant impact on the construction of the subject. For Jameson, traditional philosophical and psychological models set up a 'conception of the subject as a monadlike [sic] container' (1991: 15). This description of the subject has two key aspects: as a monad it acts as an entirely discrete, individual unit, and as a container it is a vessel for forces operating from within. Jameson uses Edvard Munch's famous painting, *The Scream*, as an example of the terrible price of individualistic self-sufficiency – a scream of 'atrocious solitude and anxiety' – representative of the psychic states of 'radical isolation' (1991: 14) and alienation to be found in the era of high modernism. Freud's concepts of hysteria and neurosis utilise the model of the subject as a vessel, a container of unconscious desires, memories and traumas, which constitute the hidden, inner depths of the self. It is this conception of the subject that Baudrillard undermines utilising the figure of the hologram to offer a narrative in which the inner depths of the self are made manifest and visible, marking the end of the unconscious mind and a celebration of transparency. By contrast, Jameson offers a historical analysis whereby changes to the construction of the subject, such as the shift away from the model of the monad/container, are said to be reflected by a 'shift in the dynamics of cultural pathology' (ibid.) in which the alienation of modernism gives way to the fragmentation of the postmodern.

If Baudrillard characterises the postmodern subject in terms of transparency and visibility, Jameson focuses on fragmentation and temporal breakdown, drawing on the psychopathology of schizophrenia. While he utilises Jacques Lacan's clinical definition of schizophrenia, Jameson is careful to present his deployment of the term 'as description rather than diagnosis [and] a suggestive aesthetic model' (1991: 26). Lacan defines 'schizophrenia as a breakdown in the signifying chain' (ibid.). His account draws on Ferdinand de Saussure's definitions of the signifier, the form or sound of a word, and the signified, its content or meaning. Importantly, there is no direct, 'one-to-one relationship between signifier and signified', instead, meaning – the signified – is created through 'the movement from signifier to signifier' (ibid.), which forms the signifying chain. The movement is conducted according to organised patterns of relations between signifiers (such as binary opposition) which construct and create the 'meaning effect'. Schizophrenia occurs where there is a breakdown of the patterns of movement between signifiers thereby snapping the links of the signifying chain and resulting in 'a rubble of distinct and unrelated signifiers' (ibid.).

The link between language and subject construction lies in temporality. The signifying chain is created through temporal sequencing, 'the past, present, and future of the sentence' (1991: 27), just as 'personal identity is … the effect of a certain temporal unification of past and future with one's present' (1991: 26). Thus, as the signifying chain is broken into disconnected links, so 'the schizophrenic is reduced to an experience of pure material signifiers, or, in other words, a series of pure and unrelated presents in time' (1991: 27). Outside of linear temporal sequencing, the 'present suddenly engulfs the subject with undescribable [sic] vividness' (ibid.). The description emphasises the powerlessness of the postmodern subject, its inability to sequence, organise and thereby control information. This is an extreme vision of fragmentation in which the subject becomes nothing more than an aggregate of discontinuous signifiers.

Jameson's conception of schizophrenia as an aesthetic strategy is less disjunctive. The 'isolated signifier is no longer … an incomprehensible yet mesmerizing fragment of language but rather something closer to a sentence in free-standing isolation' (1991: 28). In functioning as a sentence, there is a sense of meaning being created amid the fragments. Rather than focusing on temporal disjunction, Jameson views the aesthetics of fragmentation as offering new modes of syntagmatic relations – the juxtaposition of signifiers creating unexpected connections between them – summed up by the slogan 'difference relates' (1991: 31). The postmodern viewer is thus compared to David Bowie's character in *The Man Who Fell To Earth* (Nicolas Roeg, 1976) 'who watches fifty-seven television screens simultaneously' (ibid.). Jameson suggests that such a viewer must 'rise somehow to a level at which the vivid perception of radical difference is in and of itself a new mode of grasping what used to be called a relationship: something for which the word *collage* is still only a very feeble name' (ibid.). However, this brief, positive analysis of the ways in which the surface structures of syntagmatic relations might constitute new forms of 'textual play' is couched in highly tentative terms, forming an unstable counterpoint to Jameson's typically negative depictions of postmodern aesthetics (1991: 12).

Many of Jameson's accounts of postmodern aesthetics trace the trajectory from modernism to the postmodern, constructing it as a narrative of decline. He famously traces the shifting constructions of both art object and artist by comparing and contrasting Vincent van Gogh's painting *A Pair of Boots* with Andy Warhol's picture *Diamond Dust Shoes*. The van Gogh painting takes the viewer to an 'initial situation' comprising 'the whole object world of agricultural misery, of stark rural poverty, and ... backbreaking peasant toil, a world reduced to its most brutal and menaced, primitive and marginalized state' (1991: 7). Thus the painting is grounded in a material reality. Deploying a Nietzschean model of the artist as overman, Jameson reads the act of painting as a 'willed and violent transformation of a drab peasant object world into the most glorious materialization of pure color in oil paint' (1991: 7). The painter thus acts as a subject who wills change in the object, the sheer force of his personal vision presented by the extent to which the art work transforms its initial material grounding. The transformation wrought by van Gogh is a 'Utopian gesture [that produces] a whole new Utopian realm ... of that supreme sense — sight ... which it now reconstitutes for us as a semi-autonomous space in its own right, a part of some new division of labour in the body of capital' (ibid.). Importantly, the utopian gesture is conceptualised as opening up a new 'semi-autonomous' space, a space outside the regime of monopoly capitalism, which creates the possibility of the delineation of new forms of socio-economic organisation.

In contrast, Warhol's *Diamond Dust Shoes* has no relation to an initial situation. The photograph of the shoes takes the viewer to other images — specifically advertisements — thereby circumventing any reference to an external reality and thus presenting a 'fundamental mutation in ... the object world ... now become a set of texts or simulacra' (1991: 9). Warhol's work is both intertextual and reflexive, the photograph of the shoes stripping away 'the external and colored surface of things ... to reveal the deathly black and white substratum of the photographic negative [which] subtends them' (ibid.). This empty, reflexive gesture is 'an inversion of Van Gogh's Utopian gesture' stripping away colour rather than adding it, turning inwards rather than reaching outwards; there is no moment of transformation, the waning of colour reveals the photographic underpinnings of the 'glossy advertising images' (ibid.) that the picture references. Thus the picture does not open up any new spaces; it simply demonstrates the workings of late capitalism.

Warhol's inability to construct a transformative moment is not an individual failure to embody the figure of the artist as overman, but rather the result of his being positioned at the locus of a shift between different forms of capitalism. At one level Warhol cannot embody the individualistic agonised figure of the high modernist artist because the shift into the postmodern means the monad/container model of subjectivity is no longer viable. For Jameson, Warhol's images of Campbell soup cans, 'which explicitly foreground the commodity fetishism of a transition to late capital, ought to be powerful and critical political statements' (ibid.). Their failure to be either of these things means they demonstrate the pervasiveness of late capitalism in which 'aesthetic production ... has become integrated into commodity production' (1991: 4).

Jameson's depiction of late capitalism as an all-pervasive system strongly resembles Baudrillard's analysis of capital as a closed circuit. However, the key difference between them is that Baudrillard uses the imagery of relentless circulation to mark the end of power and politics, while Jameson resolutely refuses to give up both concepts. The difference highlights Jameson's paradoxical position as a Marxist theorist of the postmodern, analysing an economic and cultural development that vaporises the theoretical terms of his own analysis. As a political theorist, Jameson analyses the postmodern in order 'to reflect more adequately on the most effective forms of any radical cultural politics today' (1991: 6). However, he acknowledges that the traditional placement of cultural politics and theory as 'cultural acts outside the massive Being of capital' is no longer possible (1991: 48). All such theorising, 'from slogans of negativity, opposition, and subversion to critique and reflexivity', shares 'a single, fundamentally spatial, presupposition, which may be resumed in the ... time-honoured formula of "critical distance"' (1991: 48). For Jameson, the pervasive nature of global capitalism destroys all forms of distance – the very basis of critique and the conceptualisation of political/social alternatives. His tentative solution is new modes of 'global cognitive mapping', enabling us to locate our bearings while living under late capitalism, and thereby 'regain a capacity to act and struggle which is at present neutralized by our spatial as well as our social confusion' (1991: 54).

While Jameson is critical of 'moralizing condemnations of the postmodern and of its essential triviality when juxtaposed against the Utopian "high seriousness" of the great modernisms' (1991: 46), his narratives of the shift from modernist to postmodern aesthetics frequently take this form. The analysis of Warhol's *Diamond Dust Shoes* is used to define the key characteristics of postmodern art, namely: 'flatness or depthlessness [*sic*], a new kind of superficiality in the most literal sense' (1991: 9). Attention is drawn to the surface of Warhol's picture by its seal, which contains sparkling pieces of glitter, inciting feelings of 'decorative exhilaration' in the viewer. The 'gratuitous frivolity of this final decorative overlay' is contrasted with the ethical effect and emotional affect of modernist sculpture: 'the august premonitory eye flashes of Rainer Maria Rilke's archaic Greek torso which warn the bourgeois subject to change his life' (1991: 10). The condemnatory conceptualisation of the sparkling surface is evident from the logic of negation underpinning the key moves: it marks the waning of affect, the end of ethics, it fails to challenge the viewer, and fails to set up the necessary critical distance through which the viewer might review his/her life. It is the sense of the tremendous value of what is being lost that sets up the depiction of such frivolity as 'gratuitous' – an unjustified and unjustifiable superficiality.

On Jameson's model postmodern aesthetics is continually defined by loss. The end of modernism marks the decline of the individual subject and concomitant death of art as a form of personal vision. The artist can no longer be an overman who wills and transforms the material object world, becoming instead a postmodern bricoleur who recycles images drawn from a world become text. Importantly, this marks the end of the possibility of originality in aesthetic production. Jameson links personal vision to the highly individualistic styles of modernist artists such as William Faulkner and D. H. Lawrence, who 'ostentatiously deviate from a norm [displaying] their wilful eccentricities' (1991: 16). The stylistic extravagances of modernist art were once the target of parody, which drew attention to the comical aspects of their extreme divergence from linguistic norms. However, the personal vision of such modernist artists has now been reduced to style, their work offering a series of diverse stylistic options all of which are available simultaneously: 'advanced capitalist countries today are now a field of stylistic and discursive heterogeneity without a norm' (1991: 17).

The loss of any sense of stylistic/linguistic norms means postmodern art forms are characterised by juxtapositions that break down traditional boundaries, moving seamlessly between different genres and incorporating both high and low art forms. Importantly, the loss of the norm marks the end of parody, thereby ushering in the key form of postmodern intertextuality, pastiche. Jameson defines both parody and pastiche as forms of imitation; however, the latter takes a particularly debased form. While parodic mimesis locates its comedy in divergence from the norm, pastiche 'is a neutral practice of such mimicry ... amputated of the satiric impulse, devoid of laughter and of any conviction that alongside the abnormal tongue you have momentarily borrowed, some healthy linguistic normality still exists' (ibid.). The language of amputation and abnormality make the negative logic underpinning this definition absolutely clear. Famously, pastiche is defined as 'blank parody, a statue with blind eyeballs' (ibid.). The metaphor evokes 'the august premonitory eye flashes' of Rilke's statue, presenting pastiche as both maimed and inert, a form of intertextuality that *cannot* be creative for it marks the end of originality and personal vision, as well as the closure of spaces of challenge and critique.

Jameson's analysis of film as a medium focuses on nostalgia films, drawing on his conception of pastiche and relating it to the wider issue of the loss of history. Like Baudrillard, he is concerned with the remake, examining the ways in which such films offer a reconstruction of images of the past, thereby displacing and effacing the real historical past. Jameson moves beyond a one-to-one relation between the original and the remake, noting the ways in which *Body Heat* (Lawrence Kasdan, 1981) evokes numerous different versions of *Double Indemnity*: from James M. Cain's novel to Billy Wilder's film (1944). For Jameson, the multiple references of *Body Heat* reconstruct pastiche or '"intertextuality" as a deliberate, built-in feature of the aesthetic effect and the operator of a new ... pseudohistorical depth, in which the history of aesthetic styles replaces "real" history' (1991: 20).

Unlike Baudrillard, for whom the remake demonstrates a process of perfecting the image, emphasising its flawlessness, Jameson constructs the remake as a transition into fashion and style, emphasising its superficiality. Thus the nostalgia film reconstructs the past 'through stylistic connotation, conveying "pastness" by the glossy qualities of the image, and ... "1950s-ness" by the attributes of fashion' (1991: 19). Such films are symptoms of a wider cultural crisis, namely, the loss of history and our subsequent inability to construct a sense of the present as a historical epoch. Approaching 'the present by way of ... the pastiche of the stereotypical past, endows ... present history with the spell and distance of a glossy mirage' (1991: 21). In reconstructing the past, the nostalgia film effectively erases the time line of past, present and future.

Jameson does attempt to delineate a more positive category of 'post-nostalgia' films, which are said to open up the possibility of 'some properly allegorical processing of the past' (1991: 287). He reads *Something Wild* (Jonathan Demme, 1986) as 'an essentially allegorical narrative in which the 1980s meet the 1950s' (1991: 290). The film begins with Lulu (Melanie Griffith) abducting Charlie (Jeff Daniels), a married, yuppie type, whom she inveigles into adultery and small-time criminality. They journey to her maternal home, where 'Lulu' is revealed to be Audrey, and the couple attend her class reunion. However, Audrey's attempt to pass off herself and Charlie as an ideal married couple is disrupted by the arrival of Ray (Ray Liotta), her estranged, abusive, ex-convict husband. Ray reveals Charlie has lied about being married; he is in fact divorced, and persuades Audrey to return to him. Charlie then rescues Audrey from Ray and the pair travel to his home, where Ray finds them, subjecting both to violent assault before being killed by Charlie.

Jameson's allegorical reading positions the three key characters as emblematic of particular decades. Thus Ray is read as 'a simulation of the fifties', his costume and hairstyle evoking 'romantic representations of ... rebellion, in the films of Brando and James Dean' (1991: 291) He is also a simulation of a gothic villain offering 'a representation of someone *playing at being evil* ... his malevolence ... as false as his smile' (1991: 290). The language of simulation situates Ray's '1950s-ness' at a distance from the reality of the historical era, which would be properly configured as a series of historical events or counter cultural movements. The confrontation between the 1950s and the 1980s is that of Ray versus the corporate yuppie Charlie and is staged via the figure of Lulu/Audrey who is read as a symbol of a reconfigured 1960s – 'seen [through] alcohol rather than drugs' (1991: 292).

Jameson's analysis of Lulu/Audrey overlooks the references to the 1920s indicated by the character's initial choice of hairstyle and alias. Thus Audrey is first seen sporting a black jaw-length bob with a straight eyebrow-skimming fringe, referencing Louise Brooks in *Pandora's Box*

(Georg Wilhelm Pabst, 1929); indeed, she adopts the name of the star's character in that film, Lulu. Her black clothing draws on the styles of the mid-1980s, the top featuring the ubiquitous shoulder-pads, while her accoutrements reference the ethnic styles of Zandra Rhodes. Audrey's appearance changes dramatically across the film: from an initial appearance as Louise Brooks, to the adoption of a figure-skimming, Monroesque, white prom dress for the class reunion, to a final vision of Princess Diana-inspired respectability in a demure polka-dot dress complete with white cocktail hat and gloves. For Jameson, Audrey's erratic behaviour – from kidnapping to conformity – is 'organized around sheer caprice'; 'the costume changes lend this … purely formal unpredictability a certain visual content; they translate it into the language of image culture and afford a purely specular pleasure in Lulu's metamorphoses (which are not really psychic)' (1991: 292).

Jameson's reading of Lulu thus constructs her as a pure surface devoid of any psychic depth. It is therefore surprising that she is presented as the key term in his semiotic square of the film's narrative structures. Moreover, Jameson's deployment of a mode of textual analysis that aims to 'identify "the elementary structures of signification" … underlying culturally meaningful narratives' (Elsaesser & Buckland 2002: 33) also constitutes a reversion to depth hermeneutics that seems oddly out of place. Jameson's semiotic square of the narrative logic of *Something Wild* positions the unpredictability represented by Lulu as the primary, positive term. This is pivoted against its opposite, crime, and its contrary, predictability, forming a square comprising four key terms: unpredictability, crime, predictability, non-crime. Lulu represents the matrix of unpredictability through which Charlie must pass in order to 'differentiate [him] from his fellow yuppies by making him over into a hero or protagonist of a different generic type than Ray' (1991: 293). Charlie's increasingly informal costuming – from executive suit to t-shirt and shorts – is read as indicative of his character's metamorphosis. However, given Jameson's general equation of fashion and glossy superficiality, it is unsurprising that the changes wrought in Charlie are ultimately insufficient to create a new type of hero. Indeed, Jameson acknowledges Charlie also fails to gesture towards new forms of socio-economic organisation – while he does abandon his corporate job at the end of the film 'it would probably be asking too much to wonder what he does or can become in its stead' (ibid.).

Jameson concludes that both *Something Wild* and *Blue Velvet* (David Lynch, 1986) 'show a collective unconscious in the process of trying to identify its own present at the same time that they illuminate the failure of this attempt, which seems to reduce itself to the recombination of various stereotypes of the past' (1991: 296). Thus the sole distinction between the post-nostalgia film and the nostalgia film is that the former overtly fail to delineate the present, while the latter unwittingly obliterate it. Importantly, Jameson's analysis of *Something Wild* constructs it as pure postmodern pastiche. The film's characterisation is presented as the perpetuation or simulation of stereotypes and its underlying semiotic structures are constructed as a play of depthless surfaces. This shift to the surface constitutes a voiding of signification, which, in turn, serves to underpin the film's inability to create new forms of characterisation or gesture towards new socio-economic structures.

Jameson's reading of *Something Wild* demonstrates the problems that arise when the foregrounding of the surface so prevalent in postmodern aesthetics is simply conceptualised as an obliteration of depth. The logic of negation that structures Jameson's overarching aesthetic model prevents him from capitalising on his own positive insights – for example, the previously mentioned fragmentation as '*collage*' (1991: 31). He notes the contradictory characterisation of Lulu/Audrey but fails to consider the ways in which Melanie Griffith's 'wild child' star persona offers intertextual reinforcement of her initial appearance as Lulu. Indeed, the kidnapping of Charlie can be seen as a star moment that works against the overarching logic of containment played out by the character's transition from law-less Lulu to domesticated Audrey. Such small, fragmentary moments of disruption resulting from complex relations between images simply cannot be mapped using Jameson's aesthetic model. The postmodern text as image is predefined as empty and superficial.

Given the obvious limitations of viewing Hollywood cinema through such a negative frame, the dominance of Jameson's work within the small field of postmodern Film Studies requires explanation. It is partly due to the apparent congruence of Jameson's position and Nöel Carroll's writing, indeed the two are occasionally combined to create the history of Hollywood style discussed in chapter one (see Garrett 2007; Constable 2014). Jameson is also one of the few major postmodern theorists who provides an extensive definition of postmodern aesthetics and repeatedly applies it to film, thereby offering a more readily accessible model for film theorists and cultural critics. While numerous individual articles draw on Jameson's theory, currently the only book-length study is M. Keith Booker's *Postmodern Hollywood*. My analysis will examine Booker's adaptation of Jameson's position and will focus on his readings of mainstream Hollywood films. I will show how Booker's popularised version of Jameson exhibits and exaggerates many of the major problems of this nihilistic conception of postmodern aesthetics.

Popularising Jameson

Booker explicitly presents his work as a popularisation and simplification of Jameson's position (2007: xviii). The postmodern is defined as 'the "cultural logic" of late capitalism, *directly expressing* its characteristics in aesthetic form' (ibid.; emphasis added). The quotation fuses the economic and the aesthetic, straightforwardly collapsing the relations between base and superstructure, and thereby taking Jameson's argument to its logical conclusion. The two major aesthetic features of postmodern film are pastiche and fragmentation. Booker shifts aspects of Jameson's analysis of postmodern aesthetics, attributing key characteristics, such as the waning of affect, to the condition of late capitalism. He follows Jameson in presenting contemporary global capitalism as increasingly all-pervasive, defining postmodernism as 'the cumulative effect of a number of continuous historical processes associated with the gradual globalisation of capital and the increasing penetration of consumerist practices into every aspect of daily life' (2007: 50). Thus, like Jameson, he wrestles with the issue of spaces outside capitalism in which to locate the possibility of critique as well as the major issue of what is to constitute proper critique.

Booker reworks Jameson's distinction between van Gogh's *A Pair of Boots* and Warhol's *Diamond Dust Shoes*, offering a film-based comparison between Frederico Fellini's *8½* (1963) and Tim Burton's *Edward Scissorhands* (1990). However, unlike van Gogh's painting, Booker does not position Fellini's film as emblematic of high modernism, instead placing *8½* on the cusp between modernism and the postmodern (2007: 33, 138). The two contrasting films are used to demonstrate the waning of affect within the postmodern. The semi-autobiographical nature of Fellini's film is said to enable the viewer 'to feel a heart behind' the images (2007:

32). The sense of emotional substance, initially provided by the director, is then shifted to the film's main protagonist: 'Fellini's Anselmi may be unable to love, but he seems to feel genuine emotions (and is a genuinely tormented human artist)' (2007: 33). In contrast to Anselmi, Burton's titular protagonist Edward Scissorhands 'is almost entirely lacking in emotional depth, is all surface' (ibid.). Thus the waning of affect, here understood as a loss of 'genuine' emotion, is intrinsically linked to the process of becoming surface. For Booker, the tortured depths displayed by Fellini's protagonist conform to the distinctive cultural pathology of modernism: 'Anselmi's predicament ... is alienation' (ibid.). In contrast, the sheer superficiality of Johnny Depp's performance as Edward Scissorhands means that alienation is no longer a possibility.

For Booker, Depp's role as Willy Wonka in Burton's *Charlie and the Chocolate Factory* (2005) equals the superficiality of his performance in *Edward Scissorhands* (2007: 33, xiii). In a departure from Roald Dahl's book from 1964, *Charlie and the Chocolate Factory* briefly charts Wonka's relationship with his father – a controlling, chocolate-hating, dentist. Booker argues that this childhood trauma is not evident in Depp's performance of the adult Wonka; there are no lapses suggesting unconscious depths. Instead, Wonka's overtly eccentric mannerisms foreground his oddness, reducing him to his economic role: 'all surface and no depth, his entire life consisting of his economic function as a designer and producer of sweets' (2007: xiii). In addition, the 'stunning array of images that constitute the interior of [Wonka's] factory' (ibid.) means that the film simply acts as a display cabinet for global capitalism.

Booker argues that the spectacular images presented by *Charlie and the Chocolate Factory* overwhelm and erase its moral messages. Key themes such as the value of family, the evils of gluttony, and the dangers of spoiling children appear 'half-hearted and obligatory' (ibid.). He connects this to the poststructuralist erasure of long-standing binary oppositions, such as good and evil, and the concomitant rise of moral relativism 'in which no point of view can be maintained as absolutely superior to any other' (2007: xvi). It is worth noting that in this account perspectivalism is simply equated with the destruction of all moral values. The equation of becoming surface with the loss of all value plays out a similar move to Nietzsche's figure of the Shadow for whom the loss of depth of meaning also marked the end of all objective values. While both Jameson and Baudrillard equate the move to the surface with the end of ethics, Booker's account of the dangers of moral relativism is closer to a general consensus within sociological criticism in which the waning of ethics is seen as a defining feature of the era of postmodernity (Boggs & Pollard 2003; Denzin 1991).

Following Jameson, Booker argues that the two key features of postmodern film are pastiche and fragmentation. The rise of pastiche in Hollywood is attributed to the 'increasing tendency in the second half of the twentieth century for films to base themselves on other films' (2007: 90). Filmmakers such as Brian De Palma and Quentin Tarantino are positioned as exemplary purveyors of postmodern pastiche, which is defined as 'rummaging through the styles of the past for usable images' (ibid.). While Jameson deploys the terminology of bricolage and collage, Booker prefers the homelier image of stew (see, for example, 2007: 28, 48, 63). Tracing the many intertextual references structuring De Palma's *Phantom of the Paradise* (1974), Booker describes the film as 'a complex postmodern intertextual and intergeneric stew' (2007: 63). Importantly, in repeatedly referencing films and other cultural forms, postmodern art shifts away from the representation of reality.

Booker links pastiche to another key feature of postmodern aesthetics in that films about films, or more specifically filmmaking, demonstrate high levels of reflexivity. Fellini's *8½* is presented as a key precursor of this reflexive aspect of postmodern style (2007: 137–8). De Palma's films are examined for offering both pastiches of Hitchcock and reflexive presentations of filmmaking. *Body Double* (1984) begins with an opening scene from *Vampire's Kiss*; however, the moment of the vampire's awakening is ruined by the actor's claustrophobia. As Jake Scully (Craig Wasson) reacts badly to the enclosed confines of the coffin, so the scene within *Vampire's Kiss* is revealed to be a film within a film. Booker notes that this reflexive structure is utilised at the beginning of a number of De Palma's films: 'Thus, when Scully later, Peeping Tom-like, observes a murder, the obvious Hitchcockian referent is *Rear Window* [1954], but the scene also derives from *Blow Out* [Brian De Palma, 1981] and ... *Sisters* [Brian De Palma, 1973]' (2007: 131). In this instance, self-pastiche adds to the spiral of reflexivity, presenting the spectacle of 'De Palma ... doing De Palma *doing* Hitchcock' and resulting in a tone of parodic 'near-campiness' (ibid.).

Interestingly, the development of De Palma's oeuvre is rarely read positively. For Carroll the trajectory of De Palma's work offers a paradigmatic demonstration of the demise of expressive allusion and the rise of empty stylisation within new Hollywood (1982: 73–4). Booker's readings set up a contrast between the complex satire of the music industry orchestrated through the network of references in *Phantom of the Paradise* and the 'entirely superficial and even gratuitous' plethora of references within *Body Double* (2007: 131). The way in which allusion works in the latter – as a series of distractions rather than a means of exploring a broader theme – is taken to be typical of intertextuality within postmodern film. Booker's analysis of postmodern intertextuality can therefore be seen to parallel Garrett's three-stage model of allusion explored in chapter one. Both present the allusive postmodern film text as the end point of an overarching narrative of decline.

Booker's characterisation of postmodern pastiche as a failure to engage in meaningful quotation is most obvious when he considers the deployment of high cultural references in Hollywood films. He contrasts James Joyce's *Ulysses* with the Coen brothers' *O Brother, Where Art Thou* (2000), focusing on their use of references to Homer's *Odyssey*. The former offers an ironic, 'incongruous juxtaposition [of] the epic world of ancient Greece and the prosaic world of colonial Dublin' (2007: 145) thereby subverting the epic form and challenging traditional literary hierarchies; the latter's attempts to parallel ancient Greece and the Depression South do not constitute 'a genuine dialogic engagement' (ibid.) but offer *mere* allusion 'pointing toward Homer while engaging him only in an entirely superficial way' (2007: 146). Booker's account of postmodern quotation as insubstantial gesture rather than genuine dialogue follows the logic of Jameson's earlier analysis of the deployment of popular sources in modernist and postmodern texts (1983: 112). In both cases, the postmodern text is deemed to fail to quote properly. Moreover, the terms through which it is judged to fail are set by key works of high modernism that demonstrate the proper use of quotation, namely its deployment in the formulation of dialogue and/or critique.

Booker's analyses of the deployment of high cultural references in Hollywood films link pastiche and fragmentation. His reading of the biblical references in Tim Burton's *Batman Returns* (1992) focuses on two features of the villain Penguin, who, 'monstrously deformed at ... birth, is placed in his basket, Moses-like, in a small "river" ... Then 33 years later, *à la* Christ, he emerges from obscurity to pursue his mission' (2007: 115). These allusions do not cohere to create a sustained level of symbolism; instead they operate 'like the images of the film to create isolated and fragmentary effects'; this means that tracing the references simply provides 'pleasure to audiences who can congratulate themselves on catching the allusion' (ibid.).

Booker's version of the entirely fragmented postmodern text takes up Jameson's analysis of the centrality of schizophrenia within the postmodern. However, the textual presentation of the fragmentation that characterises postmodernity, exemplified by Baz Luhrmann's *Moulin Rouge* (2001), is superficial and empty: 'fragmented and frenetic MTV-style editing contributes to the production of a self-consciously dazzling postmodern spectacle [that is] all flash' (2007: 6–7). Booker condemns the narrative for being 'utterly banal' and the main protagonists, star-crossed lovers Satine and Christian, are 'even more clichéd than the plot' (2007: 7, 59). Interestingly, Booker's equation of fragmentation with the destruction of narrative and characterisation resembles Schatz's account of post-classical aesthetics discussed in the previous chapter. It marks a point at which a Jamesonian version of the postmodern overlaps with the formative model of the post-classical.

Booker repeatedly distinguishes between modernist and postmodern forms of textual fragmentation, resulting in an extreme definition of postmodern texts as those that *necessarily* fail to cohere. 'Modernist formal fragmentation is centripetal … in its orientation, challenging audiences to reassemble the pieces into a coherent whole, while postmodernist fragmentation is centrifugal, denying the very possibility of wholeness' (2007: 5). In this quote unity operates as a metaphor for the construction of meaning and thus fragmentation is linked to non-meaning. Unlike Jameson who sets up brief moments whereby individual fragments might convey meaning (1991: 28, 31), Booker's image of fragmentation as an explosive spiralling movement must be seen as an emptying out of meaning. This sense of the emptiness of the postmodern text combined with its essential superficiality forms a theoretical model through which the mainstream products of Hollywood cinema can only be seen as dazzlingly vacuous.

Like Jameson, Booker presents nostalgia as a key feature of postmodern texts; however, his analysis of nostalgia in film draws on a number of sources, including the historian E. P. Thompson (see 2007: 49–51). For Jameson, the nostalgia film offers a reconstruction of the past through cultural fashions and stereotypes that erases the true historical past, ultimately resulting in the destruction of the timeline of past, present and future. While Booker also emphasises the role of postmodern nostalgia in the erasure of history, he repeatedly presents it as the opposite of other 'genuine' forms of nostalgia. Booker distinguishes between 'progressive nostalgia [that has] at least some basis in authentic experiences, so [forming] part of an effort to recover a usable past' and postmodern nostalgia, which has 'no such basis in historical truth' (2007: 50, 51). The inauthenticity of postmodern nostalgia is the result of the role of culture in the formation of memories, exemplified by 'nostalgic memories of the 1950s [that] tend to focus not on the historical reality of the decade ... but on the culture of the decade' (2007: 51). Expanding Jameson, the cultural obliterates the historical and thus 'postmodern representations of the past tend to be doubly mediated because they are representations of remembered representations' (ibid.). Postmodern nostalgia becomes a copy of a copy devoid of any relation to real history.

For Booker, the postmodern is characterised by the commodification of nostalgia itself, ensuring that it becomes part of the logic of late capitalism: 'as the market system renders culture obsolete more and more rapidly, it also attempts to maximize profits by recycling earlier culture styles as nostalgia products' (2007: 51). The recreation of nostalgia as a product marks its complete severing from any historical moment and its equation with the sale of lies, offering 'memories of something that never was' (ibid.). In treating nostalgia as a commodity, Booker goes further than Jameson, completely collapsing the aesthetic into the economic. This is important because it feeds into a more general equation of commercial success with aesthetic deficiency that is evident in Booker's work.

Booker's readings of nostalgia films focus on their utilisation of music, often providing an intricate mapping of their multiple, intertextual, musical references. His analysis of *O Brother, Where Art Thou* demonstrates the ways in which the film plays out the key moves constitutive of postmodern nostalgia. The film is said largely to evoke the past through music, drawing on the authentic cultural forms of traditional gospel and bluegrass (2007: 78–9). Unfortunately the evocation of the past fuses different eras: the main theme song 'I Am a Man of Constant Sorrow' dates from 1913 while other bluegrass recordings come from the 1940s and 1950s, thereby collapsing several different historical decades into 'one simulated version of the 1930s' (2007: 80). Moreover, 'the commercial success of the soundtrack CD' affects the authentic status of gospel and bluegrass music, the film effecting 'the commodification of the very music that it sought to celebrate as untainted' (2007: 81). In this way, the film demonstrates that countercultural elements are simply swept up into late capitalism's 'all-consuming maw' (ibid.).

The personification of late capitalism as an all-devouring monster is important because it clearly demonstrates the way it can become a closed system. Booker follows Jameson in arguing that postmodern art cannot instantiate the diverse modalities of utopianism offered by modernist critique. Postmodern artists are said to work within an environment 'in which the ability to imagine genuine alternatives to capitalism has been *seriously curtailed*' (2007: 188; emphasis added). Curtailment is not obliteration, and Booker suggests critique remains possible in films made outside capitalist Western culture. Utilising a highly problematic argument from Jameson's *The Geopolitical Aesthetic: Cinema and Space in the World System* (1991), Booker contends that the third world is less affected by capitalist consumer culture and thus constitutes one of the last places in which alternative social forms can be found (2007: 18). In this way, the Mexican film *Amores Perros* (Alejandro González Iñárritu, 2000) is positioned as relatively untouched by late capitalism, enabling it to retain 'a lingering humanism and utopianism' (ibid.). In addition, Booker sets up a category of art films that aspire to modernist techniques thereby offering the vestiges of critique. This is instantiated by European art films, such as *Dancer in the Dark* (Lars von Trier, 2000) which offers a proper 'dialogic encounter' with its Hollywood source material, *The Sound of Music* (2000: 86–7); as well as overtly experimental American independent films, such as *Timecode* (Mike Figgis & Annie Stewart, 2000).

Importantly, in the vast majority of the films that he examines, Booker follows his Jamesonian framework through to its logical conclusion. The serious curtailment of critique within the postmodern is demonstrated by a series of readings of mainstream Hollywood films, of which *Fight Club* (David Fincher, 1999) is an exemplary instance. Booker concedes that *Fight Club* is critical of capitalism (2007: 37); however, he contends that it fails as critique because it does not set out any *viable* social alternatives: 'the bloody violence of the fight clubs hardly seems feasible as a means of transcending the antagonistic social relations of capitalism' (2007: 39). The oppositional mode of living presented by the film's guerrilla force has 'no ideological agenda other than pure destruction' (2007: 40). The reduction of opposition to criminality and violence in *Fight Club* is read as symptomatic: 'almost all utopian images in postmodern film are of a similarly debased ... variety, their collective impact being to suggest the impossibility and unavailability of alternatives to ... late capitalism' (ibid.).

Elsewhere Booker addresses the ways in which postmodern critique undermines itself. While *The Player* (Robert Altman, 1992) 'is relentless in its almost Flaubertian dissection of Hollywood corruption, decadence and anti-aesthetic commercialism' (2007: 148); its reflexive narrative means that it simply becomes 'identical to the commodified films it ostensibly criticizes' (2007: 149). Booker argues that the film's genial presentation of corruption means 'there is little chance ... such critique might actually lead to genuine reform' (2007: 149–50). Booker repeatedly traces the ways in which mainstream Hollywood films fail to provide a template for practical political action, in the form of changes to the industry or the day-to-day lives of spectators, thereby signalling the end of critique. Moreover, failing in this particular respect cancels out the films' other achievements, thus structuring the film readings as mini-narratives of decline.

Importantly, Booker's analysis of critique takes the form of holding postmodern films to modernist standards and criticising them for failing to conform. The parallel between *The Player* and Flaubert, as well as *O Brother, Where Art Thou* and Joyce's *Ulysses*, draws attention to the crucial role played by the products of high modernism, thereby making the logic of the argument absolutely clear. Thus, paradoxically, the take up of a nihilistic model of postmodern aesthetics, which is defined as utterly destructive of modernist aesthetics, results in the rejuvenation of high modernism, now utilised as a positively omnipresent set of aesthetic standards. The logic of negation underpinning the definition of the postmodern sustains Booker's creation of ever more negative aesthetic categories, including the 'spoof', which, like pastiche, is a failed form of parody (2007: 167). In the final chapter, films are criticised for being 'silly' rather than providing proper analyses of social problems (see, for example, 2007: 153, 167, 169, 170). The assimilation of the surface with superficiality and the humorous with the merely silly consolidates a theoretical framework in which postmodern Hollywood films are condemned to play out the demise of modernist aesthetics and necessarily seen as gratuitously frivolous.

3   AFFIRMATIVE POSTMODERNISMS

This last chapter focuses on one major postmodern theorist, Linda Hutcheon, and examines the ways in which her work challenges the nihilistic models explored in chapter two. While Jameson's work has been taken up in relation to Hollywood film, Hutcheon's literary model is only rarely considered. This chapter will show how she provides a range of aesthetic concepts that facilitate an appreciation of the many textual strategies deployed by postmodern films, thereby offering a means of escaping the self-fulfilling conceptions of textual degeneracy and emptiness set up by the nihilistic models.

The chapter begins with Peter and Will Brooker's analysis of circling narratives, setting out the ways in which their affirmative postmodern aesthetics draw on Nietzsche's model of the eternal return. Brooker and Brooker demand that their readers 'think with more discrimination and subtlety about the aesthetic forms and accents of postmodernism' (1997: 91). This chapter rises to their challenge by combining key aesthetic concepts from Hutcheon's work, including postmodern parody and complicitous critique, with the Lyotardian non-linear model of postmodern film aesthetics set up in chapter one. The chapter ends with a detailed analysis of the diverse postmodern aesthetic strategies presented by four films: *Sherlock Junior*, *Bombshell*, *Kill Bill: Vol. 1* and *Kill Bill: Vol. 2*, the last two hereafter abbreviated to *Vol. 1* and *Vol. 2*.

Full Circle

Brooker and Brooker's analysis of the initial critical dissention over *Pulp Fiction* (Quentin Tarantino, 1994) draws together a series of familiar criticisms. They focus on the controversy caused by the film's presentation of violence, noting that both critical dismissal and approval of *Pulp Fiction* are likewise couched in the language of emptiness and loss. The film is castigated for being 'empty of social and moral content', a mere 'ragbag of film references', or, alternatively, celebrated as a knowing pastiche of cinematic violence that is so resolutely intertextual it is ultimately meaningless (1997: 90–1). Brooker and Brooker argue that the terminology attests to the critics' adherence to a traditional romantic humanist aesthetic which 'requires its bad twin in order to sustain it' (1997: 90). Positioning postmodern aesthetics as a bad twin reveals the logic of negation underpinning the definitions of the familiar aesthetic categories.

Unsurprisingly, Booker's later analysis of *Pulp Fiction* as the consummate postmodern film reprises the terminology of vacuity and superficiality. However, the initial diatribe against its moral emptiness has given way to a vocabulary that provides its superficiality with a level of cultural cachet. Thus, Booker extolls *Pulp Fiction*, as 'a perfect illustration ... of pastiche' (2007: 89) and 'one of the most self-consciously cool films ever made' (2007: 13). In a shift from film to director, the intertexts are reduced to 'signs of Tarantino's famed coolness', which are then said to operate as 'in-jokes to help audience members feel cool themselves' (2007: 89). The final shift from director to audience deploys the terminology of cool to trivialise the process of meaning construction involved in tracing intertexts. At stake here is Booker's indebtedness to a Jamesonian model of pastiche in which recycling is equated with repackaging and thus demonstrative of aesthetic bankruptcy.

Brooker and Brooker's article sets up an alternative to this purely negative conception of the aesthetics of recycling, through an analysis of repetition and intertextual referencing in circular and circling narratives. Their article focuses on *Pulp Fiction's* 'episodic, circling ... structure' (1997: 91), presenting it as paradigmatic of a new form of postmodern narrative. Quoting the work of Edward Said, Brooker and Brooker suggest that postmodernity is marked by the disappearance of social and political structures that are underpinned by a model of linear narrative; thus, 'narrative which posits an enabling beginning point and a vindicating goal, is no longer adequate for plotting the human trajectory in society' (1997: 95). While for Said, this marks a closing down of options – 'There is nothing to look forward to: we are stuck within our circle' – Brooker and Brooker argue that the episodic, non-linear structure of *Pulp Fiction* constitutes a series of circling mini-narratives in which key characters, specifically Jules (Samuel L. Jackson) and Butch (Bruce Willis), 'gain new purpose and a sense of long-term direction' (ibid.). Thus *Pulp Fiction* is said to offer a model of circular repetition, which is opened out to encompass new possibilities.

Jules can be regarded as an exemplary instance of Brooker and Brooker's model of repetition as recreation. Jules' re-evaluation of his life and work is brought about by his and Vincent's survival of a volley of six bullets discharged at close range by an unknown and unexpected antagonist. The attack leaves the pair entirely unscathed, leading Jules to read the incident as a miracle. Brooker and Brooker chart Jules' transformation with reference to a key quotation that the character delivers three times across the film: Jules 'sets [out] to reinterpret the text of Ezekiel 25:17 which he customarily recites before a killing to new ends. If he has been the "evil man" ... he believes he can become the blessed man who "shepherds the weak through the valley of darkness"' (ibid.).

Brooker and Brooker's analysis of repetition and change focuses on Tarantino's recreation of generic character types, such as the hit-man and the boxer. They argue that he 'reinvents and extends these conventions, exposing their abstract "cartoon"-like rudiments, adding unexpected dialogue, fluent monologue, a concentrated intensity ... or hyperbole of character' (1997: 96). In this way, the characterisation of the pair of hit-men departs from the confines of the pulp tradition through 'the undertow of gossipy, bickering dialogue' (ibid.). The theme of being 'granted new life' thus occurs at the level of the narrative – Jules' decision to bear witness; at the level of characterisation – Tarantino's recreation of stock generic types; and finally, at level of the casting, in that the success of *Pulp Fiction* revived 'the dipping, repetitive careers of actors such as Willis and Travolta' (ibid.). Unsurprisingly, the sophisticated model of repetition and change sustains a positive analysis of audiences who trace the complex deployment of intertextual references within and across Tarantino's oeuvre (1997: 93–4).

Importantly, Brooker and Brooker repeatedly characterise their circular model of revival and reinvention in terms of affirmation (1997: 92, 97, 99).

Their 'inventive and affirmative mode' of postmodern aesthetics is said to be exemplified by the revival of Mia (Uma Thurman) after her overdose on Vincent's (John Travolta) heroin (1997: 97). Her treatment with a shot of adrenalin, which Vincent administers as though stabbing a vampire in the heart, provides a brief foray into Gothic horror that unsettles the film's generic base. Taking issue with a critical reading of the scene as demonstrative of the ways *Pulp Fiction* showcases graphic violence, Brooker and Brooker argue it offers 'the most graphic illustration of the film's theme of re-invention and rebirth' (ibid.). The inter-linking of affirmation, repetition and new life is also evident in the film's manipulation of chronology in order to 'return us to better moments' (ibid.). The revival of Vincent in the final section offers a non-linear reprise of Mia's return from the dead, thereby affording the audience the chance 'to consider from a new angle what might have been' (1997: 99). This is both an opportunity to reappraise the meaning of Vincent's life and death and an invitation for the audience to consider how they might choose to rewrite the ending of the story.

While Brooker and Brooker do not trace the theoretical underpinnings of their own circular model, their inter-linking of affirmation and repetition strongly recalls Nietzsche's concept of the eternal return. For Nietzsche, the dynamic of the eternal return is not the endless repetition of the same but rather a repetition in difference. In spatial terms, it is not the two-dimensional, dead end of a closed circle, but rather a three-dimensional circling back and forth to create 'a series of loops each of which constitute an emerging pattern, thus opening up the possibility of creating new relations' (Constable 2005: 105) between the points on the circling structures. Looping back and forth is a mode of returning to key points from different directions, thus each circling structure offers the possibility of looking backwards and/or forwards from a new vantage point. In this way, the logic of the eternal return is linked to a reviewing of the past/future, which takes the form of a shift of perspective.

Sarah Kofman utilises the eternal return in her analysis of the role of the artist, the creator of appearances, in Nietzsche's work. Providing her own translation of a key quotation from *The Twilight of the Idols*: 'appearance means reality repeated *once again*, as selection, redoubling, correction' (1988: 189), Kofman draws attention to the way in which the creation of art is a mode of repetition. This is not a mimetic model, in which art is a representation of reality; instead the creation of art is an imitation of the creative power of nature. Moreover, the relation between art and nature sets up a fundamental distinction between those appearances/ fictions that devalue nature, such as the ascetic ideals of Christianity in which physicality and the material world are devalued in order to promote a living for death, and true art 'in which appearance is willed and the world repeated ... to enhance the creative capacity ... of life' (1988: 181). The positive valuation of physicality/materiality to be found in true art is key to its affirmative power: 'art *wills for life* yet again its eternal return in difference, a dionysian mimetic power at one with creation and affirmation' (ibid.; emphasis added).

Brooker and Brooker's utilisation of the vocabulary of affirmation is not reliant on the relation to nature that underpins Nietzsche's writing on art and the eternal return. However, there is an interesting parallel between the logic of negation that characterises fictions that devalue nature and the writing on postmodern aesthetics examined in chapter two. For Nietzsche, Christianity is based on a perverse '*ressentiment* towards life', nature and materiality; 'the ascetic ideal is negative and destructive', indeed the key concept of 'the fictional, perverse world [of Paradise] is defined purely negatively' (Kofman 1988: 180, 181). At the same time, 'perversion is always also *inversion* and *reversion*', a logic that results in the formation of a closed circle thus marking the null point of thinking – an inability to generate new categories and concepts. In the same way, the definition of postmodern aesthetics as the negation of modernist and/or humanist aesthetics simply promulgates a series of aesthetic concepts that are defined as necessarily debased. Thus the ostensible lack of creativity observed in postmodern art forms is simply a reflection and expression of the nullity of the logic of *ressentiment* that underpins the negative definition of the aesthetic concepts themselves.

Brooker and Brooker's model of postmodern aesthetics is a mode of affirmative theorising that goes beyond the logic of negation in order to open up ways of appreciating and describing the aesthetics of recycling. This is not the simple substitution of the positive for the negative, a celebration of all postmodern art forms as necessarily valuable. They take up the vocabulary of affirmation and differential repetition to create a theoretical model that is capable of mapping different types of postmodern artworks. 'If some examples of postmodern art are at once scandalous and vacant, or "merely" playful, others are innovative and deeply problematising ... cultural postmodernism is various and contradictory: fatalistic, introverted, open, inventive, and enlivening' (1997: 94).

Linda Hutcheon

Affirmative theorists of the postmodern share a characteristic conceptualisation of cultural postmodernism as both diverse and contradictory (see Brooker and Brooker 1997; Hutcheon 1988 and 1989; Collins 1989). Unlike Baudrillard and Jameson, such theorists resist presenting postmodernity as a single, self-perpetuating system, whether in the form of the endless circulation/floatation of capital, power, language and theory, or the unfolding of the logic of late capitalism. Hutcheon situates the postmodern in relation to two major dominants – economic capitalism and cultural humanism – thereby avoiding collapsing it into a single system. She notes that both discourses offer different and incompatible accounts of the individual's relation to wider society: humanism presents 'the individual as unique and autonomous', capable of self-determination through choice; while economic capitalism reveals 'the pretence of individualism (and thus of choice) is in fact ... mass manipulation, carried out ... in the name of democratic ideals' (1989: 13). As a result, the de-centring of the individual subject that is said to be typical of postmodernism can be seen to have very different effects when considered in relation to the contradictory constructions of the individual offered by the two discourses. In this way, conceptualising postmodern culture as a plurality of incompatible and conflicting discourses means that any postmodern theoretical move can be understood in a variety of ways and thus, in turn, each move also initiates a myriad of unexpected effects.

Contradiction plays a central role in Hutcheon's analysis of the postmodern: 'postmodernism is a fundamentally contradictory enterprise: its art forms (and its theory) at once use and abuse, install and then destabilize convention in parodic ways, self-consciously pointing both to their own inherent paradoxes and provisionality and, of course, to their critical or ironic rereading of the art of the past' (1988: 23). On this model, recycling is not the spiralling movement of the eternal return in difference but rather a pendulous swing to and fro in which both aspects, the repetition of the same and the differential reworking of past forms, constitute the two apexes of a single, swinging movement. This doubleness, evident in the simultaneous recapitulation and reworking of the art of the past, sustains a sense of the profoundly equivocal nature of postmodern art forms. While Hutcheon is keen to recognise the importance of both halves of the postmodern paradox of conservatism and innovation, she also opens up ways of appreciating the political and critical potential of the postmodern aesthetics of recycling.

Hutcheon's own mode of theorising draws attention to the centrality of paradox within her conception of the postmodern and the specific paradoxes that structure her own position. The symmetry between her vision of postmodern theory and her own theorising gives her writing the characteristic self-consciousness of postmodern texts. Hutcheon draws attention to the provisional nature of her position by presenting it as an addition to a long line of fictions told by key postmodern theorists, including Brian McHale, Baudrillard and Jameson (1989: 11). Unlike Baudrillard who offers a plethora of incompatible stories demonstrating the proliferation of fictions within the hyperreal, Hutcheon unfolds one particular story, her own version of the postmodern featuring doubled perspectives and equivocal texts.

Like Baudrillard, Hutcheon argues that the postmodern marks the end of viewing representation as purely mimetic. For Baudrillard, the shift away from viewing the image as a copy of the real sets up a series of alternatives, including the fourth phase of the seamless, self-referentiality of the 'pure simulacrum' (ibid.), which dissolves reality and inaugurates the hyperreal. Hutcheon stages the conflict between reality and the simulacrum in different terms, as a 'confrontation ... where documentary historical actuality meets formalist self-reflexivity and parody' (1989: 7), keeping both contrary elements in a state of perpetual play. For Baudrillard, the precession of simulacra also marks the primacy of the image seen in its defeat of other elements including reality, truth, meaning and all objective value. In contrast, for Hutcheon, the postmodern awareness of the power of images and fictions offers a different way of analysing their generative and constructive capacities, as 'systems of representation which do not *reflect* society so much as *grant* meaning and value within a particular society' (1989: 8). While Baudrillard constructs the loss of the objective ground of value as the end of all possible value systems, Hutcheon focuses on diverse, socio-cultural constructions of value. Importantly, this key shift enables her to argue that the postmodern is not synonymous with the loss of meaning and value but rather provokes discussion and analysis of how cultural meanings and values are constructed and negotiated.

For Hutcheon, the continual tension between the contrary elements of historical reality and textual reflexivity generates two key postmodern projects: 'an investigation of how we make meaning in culture', and an inter-related endeavour to '"de-doxify" the systems of meaning and representation by which we know our culture and ourselves' (1989: 18). While both projects draw on deconstructive techniques, the second is explicitly political. To 'de-doxify' is to challenge long-held opinions and beliefs, 'to point out that those entities that we unthinkingly experience as "natural" (... capitalism, patriarchy, liberal humanism) are in fact "cultural"' (1989: 2). Drawing on feminist work from many different areas of aesthetics, Hutcheon concludes that 'representation can no longer be considered a politically neutral and theoretically innocent activity' (1989: 21). Crucially, this informs her sense of the vital issues at stake in postmodern art works: 'Postmodern art cannot but be political, at least in the sense that its representations – its images and stories – are anything but neutral, however "aestheticized" they appear to be in their parodic self-reflexivity' (1989: 3). Hutcheon is thus able to avoid Baudrillard's sweeping conception of the postmodern as the end of politics because she does not simply focus on party politics (right versus left) but instead offers a feminist Foucauldian conception of the diffuse, complex interactions interlinking everyday activities with broader structures of social power.

For Hutcheon, postmodern art works have the capacity to present 'politicized challenges to the conventions of representation' (1989: 17) thereby offering a form of critique. However, the equivocalness of the postmodern text means that it cannot be regarded as purely subversive. Both 'a critique ... of the view of representation as reflective (rather than as constitutive) of reality ... it is also an exploitation of those same challenged foundations of representation' (1989: 18). The precariousness of postmodern critique is paralleled with the equivocal positioning of third-wave feminist theory: 'both inside and outside dominant ideologies, using representation ... to reveal misrepresentation and to offer new possibilities' (1989: 23). Thus both postmodern and feminist texts deny the possibility of a pure space of critique that is securely positioned outside the system. The major difference between them is that the former are deconstructive while the latter are concerned to advocate forms of political action.

For Hutcheon, the equivocal nature of the postmodern text requires theorists to maintain a doubled perspective; however, she is also concerned to challenge theorists who define postmodern aesthetics entirely negatively, such as Fredric Jameson and Terry Eagleton. Both ignore 'the subversive potential of irony, parody and humour' in postmodern artworks because they treat it as the opposite of serious art, rather than looking at the role humour plays 'in contesting the universalizing pretensions of "serious" art' (1988: 19). Importantly, Hutcheon refuses to define postmodern playfulness as simply synonymous with superficiality and frivolity: 'to include irony and play is *never* necessarily to exclude seriousness and purpose in postmodern art' (1988: 27).

Interlinking humour and contradiction, it is unsurprising that Hutcheon nominates parody as 'a perfect postmodern art form' (1988: 11). Its doubleness can be discerned in its etymology, the Greek word 'para' meaning both near/beside and counter/against, thus parody 'paradoxically both incorporates and challenges that which it parodies' (ibid.). While examples of parody from the eighteenth century are typically designed to ridicule the original, Hutcheon argues that postmodern parody has 'a wide range of forms [from] witty ridicule to the playfully ludic to the seriously respectful' (1989: 94). Her championship of parody leads her to challenge Jameson, whom she holds responsible for the 'dominant view of postmodern parody as trivial and trivializing' (1989: 113). She takes issue with his general definition of parody, arguing that it is entirely derived from the eighteenth-century model of 'ridiculing imitation' (1988: 26). This limited definition is then replaced by its opposite, postmodern pastiche, which is defined as 'neutral or blank parody ... "the random cannibalization of all the styles of the past"' (1988: 26, 27).

On Jameson's model the blank emptiness of pastiche is over-determined in that the heterogeneity of aesthetic styles available overwhelms and smothers the normative, which underpins the possibility of true parody, while, at the same time, the model of the individual subject who is able to create great works of art is no longer viable. In sharp contrast, Hutcheon argues that postmodern parody questions 'our humanist assumptions about artistic originality and uniqueness' (1989: 93). Thus, importantly, parody is not linked to a model of Romantic authorship – a send up of the truly individual styles exhibited by the great modernists – but instead is seen as a mode of writing in which the very concept of an individual style is itself questioned and contested. Parody is not linked to a set of norms – against which the individual stylistic tics of modernist authors can be sent up – but rather to a broad history of prior texts that it both evokes and reworks at the same time. Thus, for Hutcheon, parody is critical, historical and political: 'a value-problematizing, de-naturalizing form of acknowledging the history (and through irony, the politics) of representations' (1989: 94).

Hutcheon's insistence on the historicity of postmodern parody is clearly intended to challenge Jameson's account of postmodern aesthetics as nothing more than the 'value-free, decorative, de-historicized quotation of past forms' (ibid.). She argues that Jameson's analysis of the nostalgia film as purely destructive of the real historical past is reliant upon a specific definition of 'Marxist History' with its 'positive utopian notion of History and ... faith in the accessibility of the real referent of historical discourse' (1989: 113). Like Jameson, Hutcheon argues that History in the form of 'a naturally accessible past "real"' (ibid.) no longer exists. However, in sharp contrast, Hutcheon goes on to argue that history, in the sense of multiple and conflicting constructions of the past, is alive and well. Importantly, history is not effaced and displaced by texts, texts are absolutely crucial to its construction: 'documents, eye-witness accounts, documentary film footage, or other works of art [are] our only means of access to the past' (ibid.).

While Hutcheon challenges Jameson's account of the nostalgia film, she is indebted to his conception of pastiche as a lesser aesthetic form, utilising it for intertextual works that do not aspire to the double encoding of complicity and subversion fundamental to postmodern parody. 'Most television, in its *unproblematized* reliance on realist narrative and transparent representational conventions, is pure commodified complicity, without the critique needed to define the postmodern paradox' (1989: 10). Other examples of pastiche include the plethora of allusions to traditional film genres in rock videos and the 'vague and unfocused references' (1989: 12) to classical architecture in shopping malls. Following Jameson, pastiche is characterised as a failure to quote properly; however, the terms through which it fails are different. For Jameson, pastiche fuses the aesthetic and the economic – its banal recycling expresses the logic of late capitalism. For Hutcheon, pastiche is a failed aesthetic because it is insufficiently paradoxical, rigorously deconstructive, and/or reflexive in its mobilisation of past forms.

Like Brooker and Brooker, Hutcheon offers a *range* of types of post-modern text, from the vacant to the de-doxifying, encapsulated by the terms 'pastiche' and 'parody' respectively. While her wholesale dismissal of television is highly problematic, she does offer a broad definition of parody that is clearly applicable to a wide range of mass cultural products, including film and television: 'What postmodern parody does is to evoke what reception theorists call the horizon of expectation of the spectator, a horizon formed by recognizable conventions of genre, style, or form of representation. This is then destabilized and dismantled step by step' (1989: 114). In her analysis of film, Hutcheon utilises this definition to set out a spectrum of different forms of parody, from the light, Brian De Palma's *Phantom of the Paradise* (1974), to the overtly deconstructive, Maximillian Schell's *Marlene* (1984).

Both Booker and Hutcheon note the wide range of references utilised in *Phantom of the Paradise*, including *The Phantom of the Opera* (Gaston Leroux, 1911), *Faust* (Johann Wolfgang von Goethe, 1999) and, more fleetingly, *Psycho* (Alfred Hitchcock, 1960) and *The Picture of Dorian Gray* (Oscar Wilde, 1992). The plot concerns a demonic record producer, Swan (Paul Williams), who steals a song from composer/singer Winslow Leach (William Finley) and frames him for drug dealing. Escaping from prison, Leach is mutilated in an accident and thus becomes the phantom, haunting Swan's club, The Paradise. Recognised by Swan, Leach is persuaded to sign a contract in blood in exchange for having his music produced as he wanted, but Swan then double-crosses him. Booker views the film as a bleak satire of the music business, reading Leach's supporting act to 'The Juicy Fruits' as a send up of the 1950s nostalgia craze that took place in the 1970s (2007: 63). Hutcheon briefly addresses the ways in which the film reworks its major and minor intertexts arguing that it engages with 'the politics of representation, specifically the representation of the original and the originating subject as artist: its dangers, its victims and its consequences' (1989, 115). Her reading pieces together the diverse traditions of representation evoked by the intertexts, thereby offering a rebuttal of more extreme models of the centrifugal fragmentation of the postmodern text (see Booker 2007: 5). Importantly, Hutcheon's model allows her to trace both thematic overlaps and disparate contradictory elements; the postmodern text is thus neither utterly fragmented nor ultimately reconstructed as a seamless whole.

The humorous way in which *Phantom of the Paradise* positively bran-
dishes its references is the basis of its critical potential: 'Multiple and
obvious parody like this can paradoxically bring out the politics of representation by baring and thus challenging convention' (Hutcheon 1989:
115). *Marlene* offers a rather different mode of parody in its rigorous
deconstruction of the documentary genre. 'It opens asking the question:
"Who is Dietrich?" and the question is revealed as unanswerable' (ibid.).
The film is metacinematic in its foregrounding of the means of production,
showing the process of editing film clips and documentary footage, the
reconstruction of Dietrich's flat, and featuring a directorial commentary on
the difficulties of piecing together the available material. The commentary
is interspersed with extracts from aural interviews with Dietrich, attesting
to the director's difficulties, the elderly star offering tangential and often
entirely inconsistent answers to his questions. The reflexive aesthetic strategies draw attention to the fragmentation of the star as subject and thus
foreground the fictional nature of the humanist ideal of the coherent self
that underpins the genres of biography and documentary (see Hutcheon
1989: 115–16).

Ultimately Hutcheon's positive view of the critical potential of the range
of forms that constitute postmodern parody is reliant on her take up of
deconstructive rather than modernist definitions of critique. Her indebtedness to deconstruction is clear: postmodern parody's destabilisation of the
conventions of genre, style and forms of representation serves as a means of
denaturalising and thus questioning the status quo. This leads her to define
postmodern film, as 'that which ... wants to ask questions (though rarely
offer answers) about ideology's role in subject-formation and in historical
knowledge' (1989: 117). Importantly, the shift to asking questions enables
Hutcheon to avoid confining critique to the provision of answers in the
form of either pure utopian spaces (see Jameson 1991: 48) or action plans
of social alternatives to capitalism (see Booker 2007: 40, 148–50, 188).

The rejection of pure spaces outside the system as a vantage point
from which to conduct critique or the ideal end product of critique is central to Hutcheon's position. Critique is always conducted from the inside,
at once part of and different from the system that it simultaneously reinscribes and calls into question. This doubled positioning also underpins
Hutcheon's analysis of the relation between film and the capitalist system.
'Postmodern film does not deny that it is implicated in capitalist modes

of production, because it knows it cannot. Instead it exploits its "insider" position in order to begin a subversion from within, to talk to consumers in a capitalist society in a way that will get us where we live, so to speak' (1989: 114). This move is vital in that it sets out a key way in which mainstream Hollywood cinema might participate in deconstructive forms of critique. Moreover, this model of subversion acknowledges Hollywood's position within corporate capitalism while preventing it from functioning as the end point of discussion (an economic and textual 'bottom line'), thereby challenging the numerous analyses of postmodern films that take commercial success to be straightforwardly indicative of aesthetic and critical failure.

Hutcheon's embrace of paradox, her deployment of deconstruction and indebtedness to feminism play key roles in the formulation of her model of the postmodern. Importantly, these resources enable her to move beyond the logic of negation, providing her with ways out of Baudrillard's and Jameson's nihilistic analyses of the destruction of reality, history, aesthetics and critique. She offers an affirmative mode of theorising that is expressed through the new formulations of postmodern parody and 'complicitous critique'. Like Brooker and Brooker, she offers an affirmative model of postmodern aesthetics that provides a means of analysing and addressing a range of postmodern texts.

Re/thinking Hollywood's Aesthetics

While Hutcheon's work does provide the means for rethinking the aesthetic and critical potential of postmodern Hollywood cinema; her account of the derivation of postmodern aesthetics, particularly in relation to film, is more problematic. Her complex analysis of the development of postmodern aesthetics ultimately presents it as following on from modernism. 'Postmodernism challenges some aspects of modernist dogma: its view of the autonomy of art and its deliberate separation from life; its expression of individual subjectivity; its adversarial status *vis à vis* mass culture and bourgeois life ... But, on the other hand, the postmodern clearly also developed out of other modernist strategies: its self-reflexive experimentation, its ironic ambiguities and its contestations of classic realist representation' (1988: 43). In this quotation, key aesthetic strategies of the postmodern are presented as the legacy of modernism, and, importantly, it is this legacy that constitutes the basis of the critical/interrogative capacity of postmodern texts.

Two key proponents of entirely uncritical forms of classic realist representation are television and studio-era Hollywood films (see Hutcheon 1989: 106–7). Hutcheon builds on William Siska's analysis of 'traditional Hollywood movies about movie-making' such as *Sunset Boulevard* (Billy Wilder, 1950) and *Singin' in the Rain* (Gene Kelly & Stanley Donen, 1952), asserting that they simply 'retain the orthodox realist notion of the transparency of narrative structures and representations' (1989: 107). Siska is said to argue in favour of a modernist cinema that eschews spatial and temporal coherence and breaks down classical cause and effect narrative structures. Hutcheon's summary of his position replicates the oppositional presentation of the classical versus the avant-garde/modernist text, specifically the opposition realism/narrative versus non-realist anti-narrative, presented by E. Ann Kaplan's table of polarised filmic categories explored in chapter one. These well-worn oppositions form the basis of Hutcheon's analysis of the ambivalence of postmodern cinema, constructing it as a Derridian third term that flits across the binary divide of classic realism and modernism, subverting and reinstating the conventions of the former by deploying and amending the techniques of the latter.

Importantly, in viewing the reflexivity of films such as *Sunset Boulevard* and *Singin' in the Rain* as fundamentally contained by the conventions of realist representation, Hutcheon offers a model of postmodern cinema whose forms of parody are seen to have absolutely no relation to the reflexive and parodic structures offered by films of the studio era. The subordination of reflexivity to narrative parallels Bordwell's argument (discussed in chapter one) in which key examples of baring the device, such as the 'You Were Meant For Me' number from *Singin' in the Rain*, were deemed to be merely momentary instances of artistic motivation and thus ultimately subsumed by compositional motivation (1985: 22–3). However, it seems clear that Hutcheon's conception of light parody with its playful deconstruction of style, genre and past/present forms of representation is present in numerous Hollywood films from the studio era. It would seem more logical to acknowledge the connections between the comic deconstruction of stardom offered by the opening of *Singin' in the Rain*, where Don Lockwood's catchphrase, 'dignity, always dignity', is juxtaposed with flashbacks of his far from dignified beginnings as a knockabout stuntman, referencing Douglas Fairbanks' career, and the reflexive, intertexual satire of the music industry presented in *Phantom of the Paradise*. Moreover, both films foreground the techniques of sound recording, playing with different forms of disjunction between the speaking/singing subject (Lena Lamont and the Phantom respectively) and their accompanying voices.

Importantly, tracing connections between Hutcheon's form of light postmodern parody and the aesthetic strategies of studio-era Hollywood is not tantamount to arguing that there is no such thing as postmodern aesthetics. As argued in chapter one, adopting a Lyotardian model means that postmodern aesthetics can erupt at any point across the history of Hollywood. Moreover, Hutcheon's careful definitions of postmodern parody, intertextuality, reflexivity, and compromised critique form the basis of an affirmative postmodern aesthetic that constitutes a lens through which we can view the products of Hollywood differently. Taking up her conception of the paradoxical, compromised postmodern text offers a way of avoiding the hierarchical logic that privileges narrative at the expense of all other textual elements. Taken seriously, her model enables a tracing of the ways in which deconstructive and reflexive moments might intersect with and be developed through narrative. At stake here is a repositioning of postmodern aesthetics as the aesthetic strategies of mass culture, which recognises that the products of mass culture are capable of offering a variety of forms of complicitous critique.

Tracing a new non-linear history of postmodern aesthetics in Hollywood is beyond the scope of this book; however, I want to look briefly at two very different examples of reflexive, intertextual parody: *Sherlock Junior* (Buster Keaton, 1924) and *Bombshell* (Victor Fleming, 1933). The former offers a celebrated example of comedy created through a reflexive play with the conventional forms of continuity editing (see King 2002a: 45). By contrast, the latter is an often overlooked comic example of a film about making films. The readings will show that taking up key concepts from Hutcheon's postmodern aesthetics facilitates an appreciation of each film's complex textual strategies, enabling the first to offer a de-doxification of film spectatorship, while the second presents a deconstruction and reconstruction of film stardom.

In *Sherlock Junior* Buster Keaton plays a young film projectionist who is studying to be a detective. He gets engaged to the girl (Kathryn McGuire) only to be framed for the theft of her father's watch by a rival suitor. Failing

to capture the real thief, he returns disconsolate to the cinema and falls asleep while projecting the film *Hearts and Pearls*. In his dream, the original cast of *Hearts and Pearls* are replaced by his former fiancée, her father, their handyman and the successful suitor, who proceeds to menace the girl in the confines of her bedroom. Attempting to rescue her, the projectionist's dream double bounds into the screen world, only to be forcibly ejected by his rival. The long shot presents the film's audience, the orchestra in the pit and the entire 'celluloid' screen, emphasising the hero's trajectory across the screen's frame. This doubled framing also underscores the doubled reflexivity of the dream film of the projected film within the film.

The scene changes to an exterior shot and the hero re-enters the dream film only to find he cannot get into the house. As he turns away from the front door and walks down the central steps, there is a cut to a long-shot of the garden. His forward momentum is continued via an action match but the change of setting means he now falls forward off a centrally placed garden bench. Leaning backwards to sit on the bench, the scene changes to a busy street and he falls back off the kerb into the traffic. The abrupt

spatial transitions continue: 'walking along the road, he almost goes off the edge of a cliff; peering over the cliff, he finds himself looking close up at a lion; wandering around he is relocated into a desert and suddenly a train rushes closely past' (King 2002a: 45). There are eight cuts to different urban and natural locations from the city to the sea, finally returning to the garden and the scene fades to black.

The abrupt changes of location draw attention to the cuts, while the matches on action bring the disparate elements together to comic effect. The first transition, from the exterior shot of the house to the garden, sends up the convention of cutting from exterior to interior presented by the first two shots that are shown from the original *Hearts and Pearls*: an exterior shot of a large mock Tudor mansion and a medium shot of a man in evening dress putting some pearls in a safe. The eight cuts draw attention to their key function as a mode of ellipsis, a means of omitting irrelevant information, and foreground the work of the viewer in inferring the physical relation between spaces. While the medium shot of the safe is comfortably read as taking place inside the mock Tudor house, the unex-

pected transition from the front door step to the garden forces the viewer to search for connections between the spaces – the ornate architecture of the walled garden with its espaliered trees is congruent with the imposing doorway and steps – thereby drawing attention to the work that is required to construct connections. The next seven cuts are transitions that defy any endeavour to read the spaces as interconnected, thereby mocking the whole process. Throughout the entire series of eight cuts the first rows of the auditorium and orchestra pit remain visible in front of the screen showing the dream film. The doubled framing makes overt the dream film's reflexive deconstruction of both conventions of continuity editing and viewers' techniques of reading.

The fade out in the garden is followed by a fade in to the couple in the bedroom and the camera tracks forward so that the dream film fills the entire frame. On discovering the theft of the pearls, the father calls for 'the great detective Sherlock Holmes', who is played by Keaton. The presentation of Holmes' methodology within the house, eyeballing the suspects and declining all offers of information, is comic in its complete failure to conform to the techniques of painstaking forensic investigation and logical deduction set up by Sir Arthur Conan Doyle. *Sherlock Junior* is one of a large number of silent film parodies in which the great detective is presented as less than competent, beginning with the Mutoscope peepshow *Sherlock Holmes Baffled* (1900) (see Barnes 2002: 156).

Sherlock Junior overtly references its dramatic intertexts by changing the Dr Watson character's name to 'Gillette'. William Gillette was an actor-manager who wrote the first play inspired by Conan Doyle's characters, which was produced across America and Europe from 1899 to 1907. The play utilises two short stories: 'A Scandal in Bohemia' and 'The Final Problem', diverging from them in presenting Holmes as a romantic hero who eventually 'gets the girl', and thereby reconstructing 'the detective as hero-adventurer' (Barnes 2002: 128). Keaton's Sherlock both conforms to and departs from the heroic: a succession of accidents that showcase the star's acrobatic virtuosity enable him to rescue the daughter of the house from kidnappers but the rescue mission ends with both of them floundering in a lake once their car/boat sinks. William Gillette himself played the role of the great detective at the age of 63 when the play was transferred to the screen in *Sherlock Holmes* (Arthur Berthelot, 1916). *Sherlock Junior* evokes and reworks the now lost earlier film by presenting the character of Gillette as an older man who is a master of disguise and demoting him to the role of assistant. Thus the film deploys its intertexts to both evoke and displace another Sherlock, constructing a succession in which William Gillette's Holmes is surpassed by the youthful exuberance and physical virtuosity of Keaton's Sherlock Jr.

The film's final scene recalls the reflexivity of its formal play with the conventions of editing. Awakened from his dream, the hero is reunited with the girl who has successfully proved that he did not steal her father's watch. There is a cut from a long shot of him standing beside her in the projection booth to a medium shot of him looking out through the framed window of the projection box towards the film, now playing the original *Hearts and Pearls*. The hero looks directly into the camera, towards the viewer, seeking inspiration from the film. There is a cut to a long shot of the auditorium and the film within the film in which a young couple are also reconciling and the girl's partner leans towards her and pats her hand. This is followed by a medium shot of the projectionist noting the moves admiringly and proceeding to perform the same actions. The pattern of shot/reverse-shot continues as the awkward and inexperienced hero follows his debonair on-screen counterpart: kissing the girl's hand, placing a ring on her finger and finally kissing her. Keaton imitates all the gestures to comic effect, swinging his shoulders from side to side to indicate youthful embarrassment and almost doing a double take at the thought of enacting the kiss, which takes the form of a very brief, chaste peck on the mouth.

The mimetic model of life comically imitating art is complicated by the framing of the medium shots in which Keaton appears to look directly at the audience, incorporating them within a relay of gazes and thereby adding a further level of mimesis in which the real viewers might also imitate the filmic character's imitation of art. The complex mimetic model is abruptly shattered by the last shots from *Hearts and Pearls*. The on-screen couple embrace and there is a fade to black followed by a fade in on an established family comprising mother, father and two children. The following shot of the hero shows his complete bafflement at this unforeseen turn of events, foregrounding his inability to immediately imitate it! The film thus reinscribes and calls into question the adequacy of the mimetic model as a means of analysing film spectatorship. The foregrounding of ellipsis in the final fade out and fade in explicitly draws attention to what is not shown, recalling the earlier sequence of cuts and summarising the film's utilisation and deconstruction of the conventions of editing. Importantly, *Sherlock Junior* is both comic and thought-provoking, utilising reflexivity, doubling and intertexts to offer a most enjoyable parody of Holmes and to deconstruct the means of representation.

Bombshell offers a deconstruction and reconstruction of stardom in its overtly reflexive presentation of the sex symbol, platinum blonde Jean Harlow in the role of 'It Girl' film star Lola Burns. The fast-paced comedy explores the role of fan magazines and the media in the construction of stardom, referencing and parodying MGM's campaigns for Harlow. The opening montage sequence displays newspaper headlines featuring the private life of Lola, magazines such as *Photoplay* and *Modern Screen* piling up hot off the printing press, and commercial tie-ins, including hosiery, face powder and perfume, linking the star's image to the women who pur-

chase and use the products. The frequent showers of gold coins consoli-
date the clear presentation of the star as commodity. The use of two brief
clips of Harlow embracing Clark Gable incorporates the star's films within
the repertoire of the fictitious Lola.

The film footage is intercut with a series of close-ups of its spectators, each of whom is shown with their head slightly tilted to one side
gazing coyly upwards at the embrace unfolding on the screen. The range
of spectators, women and men, from adolescent to elderly, shows a vast
fan base; while their identical worshipful attitudes construct Lola as a
screen goddess. There is a wipe across the screen and a crane shot up to
an apartment window followed by two dissolves, the dream-like transition
linking a medium close-up of a young woman with a close-up of a male
fan both day-dreaming about Lola. There is a third dissolve to a long shot
of an exotic locale where satin-clad Lola is reclining on a low chaise, her
lover seated on the floor beside her, while behind them a black servant
waves a huge white feather fan. Two further shots of day-dreaming fans
are superimposed over the long shot. The second fades and Lola embraces
her lover. The editing indicates that the exotic scenario is a projection
of the fans' fantasies, which both recall and send up the Orientalism of
exotic studio locales, the play on the feather fan and bright whiteness of
the star's hair comically exaggerated by an unexpected swan swimming in
the foreground.

The fans' fantasy is humorously juxtaposed with the scene that follows in Lola's mansion, depicting 'the reality' of the star's life. Lola is first
presented as entirely glamorous, her beautiful face visible as she nestles

beneath the satin covers of a huge bed, protesting about being woken at
6am. Her breakfast juice is delivered and her conversation with the new
butler, whose name she misremembers, attests to the chaotic nature of
the household. Matters worsen with the arrival of a trio responsible for preparing her for the day's shoot, the hair-dresser and make-up artist talking
continuously while attempting to do her hair and make-up simultaneously.
Pulled in two different directions, Lola sits in the centre of the bed endeav-
ouring to finish her juice, which spills all over her negligee. The final shot
of the scene shows her far from glamorous: covered in juice, half made up
with her hair falling all over her face.

The first scene contains numerous references to Harlow's screen roles.
The introduction to Lola in her bed recalls the presentation of Harlow's
character, Kitty, in George Cukor's *Dinner at Eight* (1933). The telephone
conversation with Lola's secretary, Mac (Una Merkel), in which she reiter-
ates the director's instructions for Lola to wear 'the white dress without
the brassiere' overtly references well-known aspects of Harlow's costuming, beginning with her breakthrough film *Hell's Angels* (Howard Hughes,
1930). In *Platinum Blonde* (Frank Capra, 1931) Harlow wears a series of
'tight-fitting, see-through satin gowns and nightgowns with no undergar-
ments' (Jordan 2009: 41). The most overt film reference in *Bombshell* is a
scene in which Lola goes to the studio to do retakes on *Red Dust* (Victor
Fleming, 1932) drawing on Harlow's performance as Valentine.

In the second scene of *Bombshell*, Lola appears in a long white chiffon
dress with matching hat. The soft drapes of the flowing chiffon accentu-
ate her lack of bra and draw attention to the movement of her breasts as

she walks down the stairs. The contrast with Lola's previous appearance, covered in orange juice, emphasises the labour that goes into creating Burns'/Harlow's star image. The division between Harlow's on-screen star persona and her – equally constructed – private persona forms the reference point for the rest of the scene. Lola's greeting to her father on finding him sneaking into the house utilises slang expressions: 'You old rooster! You've been out all night and you're still boiled!' Her forceful, Chicago-accented delivery of these lines is contrasted with the upper-class English enunciation that she puts on for the journalist, Miss Carroll (Ruth Warren), who arrives to do an early morning interview on the star's 'early life'. Lola's father (Frank Morgan) joins the interview, consolidating the sense of pretension by making improbable claims to extensive acreage in South Illinois. Susan Ohmer notes Jean Harlow's 'own "origin story" was firmly upper middle class and Midwestern. The *Los Angeles Times* referred to her as a "Kansas City Society Girl" who nearly lost all her inheritance because her grandfather disapproved of Hollywood' (2011: 176). The film's parody of the construction of an upper-class Midwestern background references and sends up Harlow's private persona, foregrounding its status as a construction.

　　Bombshell revolves around Lola's arguments with the studio's head of publicity, Space Hanlon (Lee Tracy), for his orchestration of salacious publicity to promote her role as a 'Bombshell' within the popular press. After he arranges for her escort, Marquis Hugo (Ivan Lebedeff), to be taken to jail, Lola demands that Space be fired from the studio. He visits her, claiming to have been fired, and says that he has finally provided her with publicity of which she will approve – an interview with the women's magazine, *Ladies Home Companion*. Lola rings to have him reinstated at the studio, unaware that he never actually lost his job. The incongruous shift of publicity from bombshell to champion of domestic values references the abrupt change in MGM's publicity campaigns for Jean Harlow following the suicide of her second husband, Paul Bern, in September of 1932, after two months of marriage (see Ohmer 2011: 182, 191); 'They flooded the newspapers and fan periodicals with pictures of Jean in her kitchen, pictures of her in the garden with her pets, pictures of her covered with a huge apron engaged in baking a cake' (Davies 1937: 31).

　　Lola's costume for the publicity photographs in the kitchen is a fitted mid-calf-length dress whose lines are entirely spoiled by the additions of

a huge white bow at the throat and a white apron. Her demonstration of prowess in the kitchen comprises spearing a boiled potato with a large cooking fork and wonderfully announcing: 'I just love baked potatoes, don't you?' The interviewer, Mrs Pittcomb (Grace Hayle), is entirely uncritical, telling Lola that she has conformed to her expectation of meeting a 'sweet unspoiled child'. Mrs Pittcomb then asks if Lola yearns for 'the Right of all Womanhood' and on seeing her bemused expression, clarifies: 'the patter of little feet'. Lola responds by clasping both hands to her bosom as though in prayer and gazing upwards soulfully while affirming that she does want children. The pose parodies the discourse of the sanctity of motherhood espoused by women's magazines, which is drawn from the Christian tradition.

The pose is repeated across the scene, while Lola gazes soulfully at a picture of a horse and foal. When the director, Jim Brogan (Pat O'Brien), arrives at the mansion Lola suggests that they pick up their romance, marry and have children. While enthusiastic about marriage, Jim dismisses her desire for children as a moment of theatricality. He flips the bow on her dress saying: 'What's the idea of this fancy dress costume?' and expresses a wish to film her as she takes up her Madonna-esque pose. Later, Jim returns to the mansion to discover that Lola has taken his joking suggestion that she adopt an orphan literally. He repeats his offer of marriage so that she can have a child of her own, only to be rebuffed by Lola who now wants to adopt instead, saying: 'It's different now. It's gone beyond anything fleshy!' Lola's rebuff references and sends up the Christian depiction of motherhood as a pure spiritual state beyond the material, her preference

for adoption over child-bearing foregrounds the incoherence of the ideal by taking it to its logical conclusion. The theatricality of her performance of the Christian vision of the maternal de-doxifies this traditionally natural-ised category and it is here that the film's parody is at its most subversive. At the same time, the film's presentation of the complete incompatibility of Lola's two roles, mother versus 'It girl', exhibits the polarised logic of the Virgin/Whore dichotomy. While Space's question: 'Do you think I want my bombshell turned into a rubber nipple?' continues the film's denaturalisa-tion of the maternal, it also reinforces a binary logic of feminine types, thereby demonstrating the film's compromised critique of a broad history of representation.

Space sabotages Lola's endeavour to adopt by orchestrating a fight between Jim Brogan and Marquis Hugo at precisely the moment at which she is being interviewed by two respectable women from the foundling home to assess her eligibility as a parent. The fight is covered by the avidly awaiting press to whom Space suggests appropriate headlines, such as: 'Two Lovers Brawl In Burns' Home'. As the Marquis and his lawyer go to the mansion with the intention of filing lawsuits against Lola and Jim, the audi-ence are aware Space is misrepresenting the reasons for the brawl. The film thus presents the salacious publicity of the bombshell as fictitious, and by extension, suggests that the less savoury coverage of Harlow's private life following Bern's suicide, is similarly orchestrated. Lola's loss of the chance to adopt leads to an outburst in which she condemns Space, Mac and her family as 'a pack of leeches', making clear her status as a commodity that is exploited for profit. The scene links Lola's commercial exploitation by the studio and the press with her economic exploitation by both her household staff (Mac wears Lola's clothes and holds parties at the mansion) and her own family (subsidising Pops' and Junior's endless bouts of drinking and gambling). Lola resolves to withdraw her labour and disappears.

Lola flees to a spa in Desert Springs and, just like her fans in the film's first montage, pursues a romantic fantasy of escape that is based on the movies. Her new suitor, Gifford Middleton (Franchot Tone), is an aristocrat and poet, who showers her with mellifluously-delivered compliments that become ever more extravagant, the height being the wonderfully involved metaphor: 'Your hair is like a field of silver daisies. I'd like to run barefoot through your hair!' Lola's delighted response to his professions of love foregrounds their theatricality: 'Not even Norma Shearer or Helen Hayes in their nicest pictures were ever spoken to like that!' Lola and Gifford's romance meets with opposition from his highbrow, aristocratic parents, whose patent disapproval of both the movie industry and Lola's family causes it to end. The interlude parodies the language of romance presented in drawing-room comedies, the pervasive sense of theatricality preparing the spectator for the later twist when it is revealed that the Middleton family are three stage actors and the entire romance has been orchestrated by Space in order to get Lola to return to work.

The presentation of Lola's relation to capitalism is complicated in that she is both its success story, surrounded by the accoutrements of wealth, and unable to control the profits of her own labour. She is presented as a worker within the film industry and its chief commodity, her image being instrumental to the successful sales of products and magazines. Unlike Harlow's previous characters, Lola is unable to capitalise on her commodification as a sex symbol because it is presented as a construct created by the industry and the press, which she embodies (to an extent) but does not control. Thus the role of Lola differs from Kitty in *Dinner at Eight* whom Jessica Hope Jordan reads as a gold-digger who successfully trades on her sexuality to attain a luxurious lifestyle (2009: 31–3). This figure of the 'hyper-feminine woman ... utilizes commodity logic for her own personal profit *and* ... escapes the deadening bonds of conventional wage labor' (2009: 33) ultimately commodifying her own body to pursue her own pleasure. Jordan argues that both Kitty and Helen from *Hell's Angels* are examples of a contradictory combination of agency within commodification/

objectification (2009: 55–65). Importantly, both characters differ from Lola in having clearly demarcated goals and a consistency of purpose. While Lola's costumes, such as the long white chiffon dress, present her as a sex symbol, she is utterly capricious and her admirers are not in thrall to her but pursuing their own schemes: the Marquis is after her money, 'Gifford Middleton' wants a debut in pictures and even Space wants the studio to continue making a profit. Thus the reflexive presentation of the sex symbol within the industry and the farcical comic narrative creates a character who enjoys more success and less agency than Harlow's previous roles.

The film offers a complex deconstruction and reconstruction of Harlow's star persona. It draws on the intertexts created by publicity to send up the star's upper middle class 'origin story'; at the same time Lola's rejection of the Middletons and reconciliation with Pops and Junior reaffirms her working-class origins, which are typical of Harlow's on-screen characters. *Bombshell* sends up the fans' vision of the star as exotic goddess, positioning Lola alongside her fans as a worker within a large industry who escapes work via a romantic fantasy constructed by and through the movies. The fake romantic interlude also invests Lola's and Space's relationship with a level of integrity, their banter and arguments are typical of the 'lively and combative style of screwball' (King 2002a: 56) and thus indicate their compatibility. Harlow's shift from narratives of seduction into screwball met with very positive reviews. The *Atlanta Constitution* praised her performance, saying 'her first opportunity at almost unadulterated comedy and ... the platinum-haired menace is amazingly competent in the difficult work' (cited in Ohmer 2011: 187). In drawing on and sending up Harlow's image as 'It girl', *Bombshell* provides a distance from the role that enables an appreciation of the star as an actress whose fast-paced delivery and comic timing are praise-worthy. Like the circling structure of the farce in which Space and Lola reunite to fight again, the film facilitates a reappraisal of Harlow's star persona, drawing attention to qualities that are usually placed in the background: her capacity for hard work, directness and sense of humour, while reflexively demonstrating the process of deconstructing and reconstructing her image.

The theatrical presentation of feminine types across *Bombshell* de-doxifies particular ideals of femininity by presenting them as constructions. However, Lola's endeavours to embody these differing ideals, with varying degrees of success, and the shifting reconstructions of Harlow's star persona do not correspond to Hutcheon's model of extreme subjective fragmentation exemplified by the multiple and contradictory variants of Dietrich in *Marlene* (1989: 115–16). Harlow as Lola offers a range of performances of diverse forms of femininity, from motherhood to 'It Girl'. The roles are performed in a variety of ways pivoting the obviously theatrical – motherhood and the female romantic lead of drawing room comedy – against the roles that Lola/Harlow performs more successfully, those of 'It Girl', working-class girl made good, and screwball heroine. Lola's characterisation across the film relies on the viewer responding to Harlow's performance and key star intertexts in order to position some of her acts as more authentic than others: for example, working-class identity over upper-class identity, the screwball comedy with Space over the romance with Gifford. Harlow's performance as Lola in *Bombshell* can be seen as a series of acts that deconstruct and reconstruct both the character and public/private aspects of her star persona. Importantly, the shift to the surface provided by the film's foregrounding of performance is not simply synonymous with lack of depth. Harlow as Lola offers a play of surfaces that intersect and overlap thereby creating moments of authenticity.

Kill Bill

Kill Bill offers an extraordinary variety of aesthetic strategies that foreground its status as a film about film and places its female hero within a history of representation. Edward Gallafent rightly notes that the opening of *Kill Bill: Vol. 1* immediately announces its status as 'a film that will foreground cinematic techniques' (2006: 101). It draws attention to 'past and present technologies' by juxtaposing the 'fuzzy sound and wobbly image of the Shawscope and "Our Feature Presentation" screens' with the immaculately detailed black and white close-ups of the Bride's bloodied face and the 'high quality of modern sound reproduction [in] Nancy Sinatra's performance of "Bang Bang"' (ibid.). The opening also offers a model of self-conscious narration. The credits introduce the actors/stars who feature 'as the deadly viper assassination squad' in the following order: Lucy Liu as O-Ren, Vivica Fox as Vernita Green, Michael Madsen as Budd, Daryl Hannah as Elle, and David Carradine as Bill. This order initially aids the deciphering of the hand-drawn, encircled '2' that appears beneath the typed title, 'Chapter One' in that the first chapter depicts the killing of the second deadly viper on the cast list. The ending of chapter one offers the first shot of Beatrix's own list, entitled 'Death List Five', with the encircled '2' beside Vernita's name, which is then crossed out. The reflexive gesture draws attention to the re-ordering of the narrative events, O-Ren's name is already crossed out. The alignment of Beatrix's fifth Death List with the cast list suggests that the protagonist is in the process of ordering and re-ordering the narrative.

While it is possible to rearrange the narrative events of *Kill Bill* to form a chronological fabula, the division and distribution of the chapters across the two volumes invite a non-linear analysis. Indeed, Gallafent's recon-struction of the fabula draws attention to the chiming elements and his analysis of three key worlds can be reformulated in terms of the presenta-tion of the hero (2006: 103–7). Both films show Beatrix adopting the role of 'educator to instructor, or even disciple to master' and becoming the possessor of 'extraordinary powers' (2006: 107): swordsmanship and Pai Mei's techniques. These powers are particularly evident during the killing spree at the end of *Vol. 1*, and the aftermath of the failed assassination of Budd and successful killing of Bill in *Vol. 2*. The hero is presented in rela-tion to motherhood: as the pregnant bride, as the mourner of a child pre-sumed to have been born dead in *Vol. 1*, and as the mother of a living child in *Vol. 2*. The rhyming structures draw attention to the radical difference in tone of the two films, which has been noted by critics (see Gallafent 2006: 107; Booker 2007: 95).

Kill Bill abounds with quantities of intertexual references, which vary considerably in their scope and significance. Chapter two sees the arrival of the sheriff investigating the crime scene at the chapel in El Paso, played by Michael Parks in a brief reprise of his role as a Texas Ranger in *From Dusk Till Dawn* (Robert Rodriguez, 1995). The sheriff's accurate analysis of the crime scene rapidly establishes his status as a trustworthy observer. The scene presents a series of close-ups of Beatrix's face taken from the sher-iff's point-of-view. The first is green-tinted, due to the sheriff's sunglasses, and appears to present the bride in an advanced state of decomposition. The shot references *Vertigo* (Alfred Hitchcock, 1958) and the green tint used to present Kim Novak's final transformation from Judy to Madeleine (the woman Scottie loves whom he believes to have died falling from a church tower). The necrophiliac aspect of obsessional love re-emerges in the sheriff's speech as he gazes appreciatively at Beatrix's dead face:

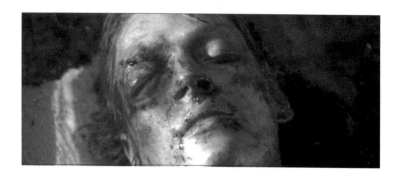

'Look at her: hay coloured hair, big eyes, she's a little blood-splattered angel.' The film cuts back to the close-up of the bride for the last three words of the speech, the words explicitly cuing the viewer to look through the splatters of bright red blood and see the dead angel beneath. This is comically undercut by Beatrix suddenly demonstrating that she is still alive by spitting blood into the sheriff's face!

The sheriff's invitation to the viewer – to look through the blood splatter and see the angel beneath – is important because it draws attention to the way in which Uma Thurman is filmed across *Kill Bill*. Gallafent draws on interview material in which Tarantino refers to *Kill Bill* as his version of *The Scarlet Empress* (Josef von Sternberg, 1934), paralleling the endless close-ups of Uma Thurman with von Sternberg's presentation of Marlene Dietrich (2006: 120). While the blood-splattered bride might seem a long way from the beautifully lit, groomed perfection of Dietrich, the close-ups combined with the verbal cue set up a particular way of reading the splatter as a veil that both covers and displays the beauty of Thurman's facial structure. *The Scarlet Empress* contains three key scenes where a veil is foregrounded to the point of almost obliterating the view of Dietrich's face beneath it: the wedding, the aftermath of the birth of the heir, and the final rejection of a former favourite. In the second, Catherine contemplates a jewel, a reward for providing an heir to the throne and there is a cut to a close-up that foregrounds the grain of the veil while drawing attention to the sculpted lines of Dietrich's cheekbones beneath. For Mary Ann Doane, the veil's play between what is seen and not seen is a model of seduction and thus 'foregrounding [its] grain … merely heightens the eroticism, makes [the woman] more desirable' (1991: 73, 74). Thurman's

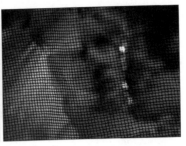

veils become increasingly dense: from the artful blood splatter of *Vol. 1* to the engrained grime of dust and mud in *Vol. 2*. While the visceral substances forming the veils do not appear to invite touch, Bill's response at the beginning of *Vol. 1* is to clean up Beatrix's face before shooting her himself, thereby combining eroticism and sadism. The references to Hitchcock and von Sternberg also serve to construct Tarantino as the latest in a long line of distinguished film directors famously obsessed with their blonde leading ladies.

Beatrix is repeatedly presented as apparently dead or near death across *Kill Bill*. The credits for *Vol. 1* end with a shot of her prone profile in silhouette against a light-coloured background, her posture and stillness suggesting she has been laid out for burial. The shifting colour palettes of the close-ups of the apparently dead angel foreground the livid contrast between the red blood and white pallor of her face in the second. The dissolve from the sheriff's bloodied face to Beatrix in the coma ward of the hospital offers yet another shift, from bright extremes of colour to subdued blue tones in which the now clean, still Beatrix appears grey, cadaverous and, if possible, even more dead. *Vol. 1* abounds in images of death that

utilise an iconography of stillness, slenderness and whiteness that can be linked to Bram Dijkstra's conception of the 'consumptive sublime'.

Dijkstra argues that the late nineteenth-century cult of invalidism flourished because the social and economic status of middle-class men was measured by the conspicuous leisure and 'helpless elegance' of their wives (1986: 27). Invalidism was the zenith of feminine helplessness, requiring considerable economic support while also indicating the virtue of the sufferer. In 'an environment which valued self-negation as the principal evidence of women's "moral value," women enveloped by illness were the physical equivalents of spiritual purity' (1986: 28). Following the equation of feminine virtue with self-abnegation, 'true sacrifice found its logical apotheosis in death' (ibid.). Artistic depictions of such women drew on a specific visual vocabulary of illness presented by sufferers of tuberculosis (1989: 28–9). The cult of the 'consumptive sublime' was signified by extreme slenderness, a languishing state of physical degeneration, and bloodless pallor (1989: 29). Dijkstra notes in passing that 'the fad of sublime tubercular emaciation ... has continued to serve as a model of what is considered "truly feminine"' to the present day (ibid.).

The presentation of Beatrix's comatose state in the hospital utilises the signifiers of the consumptive sublime, the lighting emphasising her hollowed cheekbones while the broad lines of the bed draw attention to her long slenderness. However, Beatrix's passivity is not a state of spiritual purity, but, instead, a desperate vulnerability. She is nearly assassinated by Elle and subjected to dreadful sexual exploitation by Buck who repeatedly rapes her comatose body before pimping it out to other men. One of the film's intertextual references sets up a key contrast between gendered presentations of the inactive body. Following her escape from hospital, Beatrix sits in the back of Buck's Pussy Wagon, willing her legs to work by repeating the words: 'Wiggle your big toe.' The phrase is spoken and sung to Frank 'Spig' Wead (John Wayne) by 'Jughead' Carson (Dan Dailey) in *The Wings of Eagles* (John Ford, 1957). The scene shows Spig lying on his front, looking down at a mirror to view his immobile toes. The positioning of Wayne's inactive, prone body emphasises its capacity for action, the muscular breadth of the star's famous shoulders prominently displayed. In contrast, Beatrix is shot from the front, her long legs taking up the length of the back seat, their slenderness emphasised by the loose width of the blue scrubs and her voice-over comment on their atrophied state. Wayne's body is displayed as an elegy to active masculinity, like a fallen oak, it is a reminder of lost power. The presentation of Thurman's face and body draws on the consumptive sublime, her recovery is a move away from a model of femininity based on physical degeneration and passivity.

As Gallafent notes, it is significant that the sexual violence to which Beatrix is subjected is not directly represented; the mosquito bite that wakes her acts as a metaphor for other forms of penetration, both sexual (Buck and the Trucker) and medical (Elle's syringe full of poison) (2006: 107). While *Vol. 1* foregrounds its indebtedness to films of the 1960s and 1970s from the opening credits onwards, the refusal to directly present sexualised violence runs counter to the era being evoked. Peter Krämer argues that the greatly increasing levels of sex and sexual violence in Hollywood films from 1967 onwards reached their peak between 1971 and 1973 with films such as *A Clockwork Orange* (Stanley Kubrick, 1971) and *Deliverance* (John Boorman, 1972) (2005: 55). Moreover, the containment of Beatrix's recollection of Buck's abuse to his announcement of his name and intentions means the events of chapter two do not conform to a rape-revenge narrative, a form which also emerges during the 1970s (see Clover 1992: 137). While Beatrix's attack on Buck is sequentially positioned as retribution, it constitutes a restoration of her former identity. The slow-motion presentation of Beatrix rearing from ground-level, cutting Buck's Achilles tendon, before trapping his head in the door, visually reconstructs her as 'black mamba'.

Chapter three presents the story of O-Ren Ishii's revenge on her parents' killer, the *yakuza* boss Masumoto, in the form of Japanese *animé*. The shift from live action foregrounds the mode of storytelling and the chapter offers a further meditation on the presentation of screen violence. The acutely stylised forms of blood-letting – the father becomes a geyser of blood while the mother's blood showers gently onto O-Ren's face as she hides beneath the bed – draws attention to their generic status. Writing of the mother's death, Gallafent argues that the *animé* form facilitates the provision of 'images that would be overwhelmingly vicious if presented in live action' (2006: 108). While chapter two does not directly represent sexual violence of a challenging nature, specifically the rape of a comatose woman, the shift to *animé* allows sexual and violent images 'impossible within the conventions of censorship ... the 11-year-old Oren [*sic*] astride the body of the paedophile *yakuza* boss as she kills him' (ibid.). Importantly, the shift in the mode of storytelling draws attention to the kinds of violence *Vol. 1* does represent, and the forms they take, positioning the film's presentation of violence within a history of representation.

The soundtrack for the violent deaths of O-Ren's father and mother is Luis Bacalov's melodious theme tune for the spaghetti western, *Il Grande Duello* (Giancarlo Santi, 1972). Hiding beneath the bed, O-Ren almost gives herself away with a single 'whimper' that appears as words on the screen. After her mother's death, the wailing sound of the amplified harmonica acts as a substitute for the girl's own voice, articulating her unexpressed grief, loss and desire for vengeance. The use of this musical instrument to convey a child's voice and these emotions references *Once Upon a Time in the West* (Sergio Leone, 1969), another spaghetti western, in which 'Harmonica' (Charles Bronson) pursues Frank (Henry Fonda) for killing his brother. The main difference between the films is that *Vol. 1* uses Bacalov's music to convey O-Ren's emotions in one scene, whereas Ennio Morricone's score for *Once Upon a Time in the West* provides the laconic Harmonica with an expressive voice, a mode of mourning for his brother, that grants the character emotional depth in accordance with a psychological model of trauma.

Chapter three's combination of two sets of references, Japanese animation and the spaghetti western, draws attention to the status of revenge as a cross-cultural motif while also demonstrating a key feature of the formula. O-Ren's insistent questioning as she kills Masumoto: 'Take a good look at my face. Look at my eyes. Look at my mouth. Do I look familiar? Do I look like somebody ... you murdered?!' parallels Harmonica's demand for recognition as he looks into Frank's dying face after their duel. Both films pivot the figure of an innocent child against a psychopathic villain and the absolute distinction between good and evil is crucial to the presentation of exacting revenge as entirely satisfying. However, Harmonica is presented as traumatised by the past, while O-Ren endures a brutal rite of passage into a criminal underworld where she utilises extreme violence to rise to power.

Chapter five, 'Showdown at the House of Blue Leaves', builds on and reworks previous intertextual references. The musical cue for the showdown is the theme from the television series *Ironside* (NBC, 1967–75) starring Raymond Burr as the eponymous paraplegic Chief of Detectives. It is previously used in chapter one, overlaying Beatrix's brief flashback to the vipers' attack in the wedding chapel, which prefaces her fight with Vernita.

The repetition of the theme is a narrative recontexualisation – here the allusion to *Ironside* underscores Beatrix's recovery from coma and paralysis. Chapter five also builds on the previous references to spaghetti westerns, adding Morricone's theme for *Death Rides a Horse* (Giulio Petroni, 1967), another revenge narrative in which a child grows up and hunts down the killers of his family. The theme plays as Beatrix holds Sophie Fatale captive and demands O-Ren's presence. Her entrance onto the upper landing of the House of Blue Leaves is overtly theatrical; her entourage shifting the symmetrical slatted wood and paper doors, a series of frames within frames, allowing their leader to make an appropriate entrance centre stage. Morricone's theme underpins the vital moment in which O-Ren recognises her accuser and the film cuts from a zoom into a close-up of her face to a zoom into an extreme close-up of Beatrix's eyes, referencing the visual style deployed by Leone for protagonists in the prelude to the final shootout. Importantly, the music links both protagonists as people who absolutely understand revenge and its formalities. The self-conscious play with form across the final battles draws attention to the orchestration of the *dénouement* of the revenge narrative.

The action is initiated by Beatrix lopping off Sophie's arm, which spurts blood in the geyser style of O-Ren's father, the *animé* reference foregrounding the stylisation of the violence and the abundance of gore across this sequence. The complex and lengthy battle sets Beatrix against three main waves of antagonists: the six bodyguards at House of Blue Leaves, Gogo, and the rest of the Crazy 88. These are all preludes to the final battle with O-Ren. Beatrix's comment at the end of the first wave – 'So O-Ren, any more subordinates for me to kill?' – reflexively draws attention to the structure. The first two waves have no extra-diegetic music, the magical and invincible quality of the Hattori Hanso sword is enhanced by sound effects in which the death of victims is precisely timed with the sword's movements, such as its withdrawal from the body. The different waves act as showcases for screen fighting, displaying ever more complex uses of technique, particularly wire work and gore effects. Gogo's death is indicated by a close-up displaying artfully placed blood dripping from her eyes. The focus on the eye continues during the fights with innumerable members of the Crazy 88, when Beatrix briefly abandons swordplay to pluck out the eye of one of her antagonists, the change of tactics emphasised by a shift from colour to black and white. The film shifts back to colour on an extreme close-up of Beatrix's eyes, just before the lights are switched off and the fighters continue their battle as silhouettes against a blue screen that is divided into rectangles.

The blue screen is the zenith of the visual shifts from colour to black and white, directly foregrounding the means of production. The changes of visual register act like the music, serving to distinguish the different phases of the lengthy third wave of the battle. The action is carefully co-ordinated with the extra-diegetic music, emphasising the choreography of the fighting and the virtuosity of those performing. The reduction of the characters to silhouettes draws attention to the dancing movements of the bodies, the controlled swordplay balancing the previous exhilaration of the flights facilitated by wire work. The third phase of the battle utilises every convention: from the moment of comedy when the 'last' youthful gang member is spanked with a sword to the re-emergence of the last 'dead' adversary, Johnny Mo, after the battle has apparently ended. The fight with Johnny has both antagonists precariously balanced on the rails at the edge of the balcony, from which he finally falls into a bath of blood, an obvious and comic visual metaphor for the bloodbath that has ensued. In this lengthy scene postmodern parody takes the form of homage that both deploys and deconstructs a broad horizon of conventions, satisfying generic expectations while paring down the battles to the exhilaration of pure movement.

Throughout this scene, Beatrix wears a yellow tracksuit with a black side stripe in the style of Bruce Lee in *Game of Death* (Robert Clouse, 1978). However, her successful dispatch of innumerable adversaries is far in excess of the three fights that the track-suited Lee performs at the end of the film. The duel with O-Ren in the snow garden conforms to the format of one-to-one combat in *Game of Death*, the height discrepancy of the female combatants reminiscent of that between Lee and Kareen Abdul-Jabbar. The setting of the snow garden and slower pace of the final duel draws on the *dénouement* of *Lady Snowblood* (Toshiya Fujita, 1973). The combatants hold the fighting postures, Beatrix wobbling with fatigue as she attempts to rival O-Ren's calm control. O-Ren slices Beatrix down the back, and once she has fallen full length to the ground, taunts her: 'Silly Caucasian girl likes to play with Samurai swords.' There are two close-ups of Beatrix's blood-splattered, pale face against the whiteness of the snow. In the first, her breath comes in harsh gasps, drawing on the visual and aural signifiers of the consumptive sublime. The film cuts to a side-shot of Beatrix rising up into the frame, an extreme close-up of O-Ren's eyes as she recognises the full power of the avenging adversary, and back to Beatrix as she announces: 'Attack me with everything you have.' The exchange draws attention to the formal codes of the fight, Beatrix is given time to regroup, she then attacks O-Ren successfully and accepts her apology for her earlier taunt. This duel is a game of death played out in accordance with formal

rules, the ritualised orchestration and courteous exchanges making it an absolutely satisfying revenge.

While *Vol. 1* uses a wide range of intertextual references in different ways, it repeatedly places Beatrix in relation to male heroic figures with whom she is either contrasted, such as John Wayne, or whom she resembles and surpasses, such as Ironside and Bruce Lee. The film thus engages with a history of representation in order to foreground its depiction of a female hero. In the same way, the articulation of O-Ren's determination to become an avenger through Bacalov's music draws attention to the paucity of female revengers within the genre of the spaghetti western. The presentation of Beatrix's comatose state, her slow recovery from paralysis, and moment of impending death during the final duel, draws on the signifiers of the consumptive sublime. The close-ups of her face as she lies dying in the snow are exemplary, the veiling provided by the artful blood splatter drawing attention to the beauty of the bone structure of Thurman's face. However, the close-ups are juxtaposed with the side-shot that constitutes the move into critique, the hero hauling herself back up to fight again. *Vol. 1* thus offers a complicitous critique of the consumptive sublime, repeatedly deploying its iconography in order to play out a scenario in which the female hero vanquishes the threat of enforced passivity and death, again and again.

Vol. 2 deploys its intertextual references to construct a rather different Beatrix. The first chapter, 'Massacre at Two Pines', is set in the chapel in El Paso. Moving towards the open door at the end of the chapel, Beatrix hears the sound of a flute, indicating Bill's presence. She stands silhouetted in the shadow of the doorway before moving onto the porch, looking out over the brightly-lit desertscape. The shot reprises the presentation of Martha (Dorothy Jordan) at the beginning of *The Searchers* (John Ford, 1956) – a seminal revenge narrative. In both cases the woman is placed at a threshold between two spaces, the desert and house/wedding chapel, which represent the men she loves: the outlaw and the suitable husband. The paralleling of Beatrix with Martha rather than Ethan, who is played by John Wayne, marks her repositioning as a mother figure, as well as indicating the importance of familial and other relationships in *Vol. 2*. It is notable that the remaining vipers targeted for assassination are all linked by ties that are more than professional association: Elle has replaced Beatrix as Bill's lover, Budd is Bill's brother and Bill was Beatrix's lover and the father of their child. The additional ties complicate the process of exacting revenge, making it far less clear cut, no longer a battle between equal, professional adversaries like Vernita and O-Ren. The first film has a trajectory outwards, from Vernita's home to Japan, and the spacious public arenas of the final battles. The second turns inwards, returning to the domestic and the battles take place in confined private spaces, such as Budd's trailer and Bill's hotel suite/home.

Vol. 2 deploys Morricone's music, linking Beatrix to Clint Eastwood's 'Man with No Name' from Sergio Leone's *A Fistful of Dollars* (1964). Keith Booker insists that the two characters are straightforwardly paralleled: 'Kiddo proceeds ... quietly and grimly in the mode of Clint Eastwood's nameless gunslinger, to kill off the remaining two vipers'; however, he does immediately note that the comparison rests on a misdescription of the plot as Beatrix does not kill either Budd or Elle (2007: 96). In *A Fistful of Dollars*, Morricone's 'Deguello' is used as a prelude to the final gunfight between the Rojos and the Man with No Name. The latter emerges through the dust created by exploding dynamite, the trumpet theme triumphantly announcing his return to battle, having barely survived torture by the Rojos. The music continues as the participants take up their proper places for the final battle, prolonging time before the rapid exchange of gunfire. At the end of the theme, Ramón fires seven shots at the Man with No Name, grouping them carefully around his heart. While the shots cause their recipient to fall over, they fail to kill him because of the armour plate hidden beneath his poncho. Restored to health and apparently impervious to gunfire, the Man with No Name appears invincible, shooting four henchmen in a single volley of shoots, before finally killing Ramón.

In *Vol. 2* Morricone's 'Deguello' begins after Beatrix has launched herself at Budd's trailer door, Hanso sword in hand, only to be forcibly ejected by a blast from a shotgun full of rock salt. The trumpet theme begins as Budd exits his trailer, a placing that serves to underscore Beatrix's dissimilarity from Eastwood's invincible gunslinger. The first battle of *Vol. 2* announces its marked difference from those in *Vol. 1*, the invincibility of the bearer of the Hanso sword shattered by a blast from a shotgun. The scattering of the bleeding wounds across Beatrix's chest displays her vulnerability, contrasting with the neat grouping of seven shots on the Man with No Name's impenetrable armour, while also differentiating between Budd's homemade survival tactics and Ramón's skill. Budd kicks Beatrix's sword away, and injects a sedative into her buttock, the music ending as she falls unconscious, face down into the dust. The trumpet theme thus acts as an elegy to a particular type of orchestrated showdown in which combatants duel in accordance with rules and rituals. It both recalls and marks the end of Beatrix's status as the invincible golden warrior of *Vol. 1*. The theme of loss is played out again in chapter nine, Beatrix and Elle's dirty fight in Budd's cluttered, filthy trailer contrasting with the formal duel in the beauty of the snow garden.

Budd's decision to punish Beatrix by burying her alive continues the themes of enforced passivity and death from *Vol. 1*. However, the second film offers a rather different visual staging of the process. The camerawork aligns the audience with Beatrix, showing her in profile, her tied hands clutching the torch, while the last slivers of light disappear as the coffin lid is nailed down. The screen goes black, leaving only the sound of her frenzied breathing and the arrhythmic pacing of the noise of the dirt piling up on top of the coffin. Gallafent notes the 'cinematic bravura' (2006: 113) of the staging of this episode, withholding the image to the focus on sound alone. Light returns when Beatrix switches on the torch, showing her reactions of fear, tears and fury. Importantly, her animation and lack of stillness means that this does not conform to the consumptive sublime. After the truck drives away, Beatrix's breathing slows and she becomes more still. However, this stillness is not a preparation for death, a languid acceptance of passivity, but rather a gathering of all her mental and physical resources. The reassertion of her resolve and strength is indicated by her decision to switch off the torch and face the darkness alone.

The structure of *Vol. 2* follows that of *Vol. 1* in that a moment of enforced passivity, burial alive and recovery from paralysis respectively, prefaces a flashback to past events: tutelage under Pai Mei and O-Ren's revenge. Both flashbacks provide Beatrix with the will to recover, while Pai Mei's brutal training also provides the means. Morricone's theme 'L'Arena' for *Il Mercenario* (Sergio Corbucci, 1968) begins as Beatrix embarks on her recovery by attaining the razor hidden in her boots. Like the 'Deguello' the musical theme is carried by a trumpet; however, its triumphant tones are accompanied by a snare drum, drawing attention to the military levels of discipline required for Beatrix to punch through the coffin and emerge from the depths of the earth. The shot of the clutching hand rising from the grave of Paula Schulz is clearly a reference to the end of *Carrie* (Brian

De Palma, 1976). While brief, the comically reprised intertext facilitates a welcome change of tone, which is compounded by Beatrix's appearance as a zombie in the diner.

Vol. 2 continues the meditation on screen violence offered by *Vol. 1*, extending it in a variety of ways. The staging of the burial alive in chapter eight aligns the spectator with a victim of torture, showing Beatrix's range of emotions as she suffers, contrasting with the reflexive and artful presentation of the physical effects of violence in the battles at the end of the first film. While *Vol. 1* offers a brief presentation of the vipers attacking Beatrix in the chapel in *animé* form, both films do not show the massacre of the wedding party. The second draws attention to this omission through the sweeping movement of the camera pulling out of the chapel, the vipers stepping into the frame before moving in. Thus, both the first and second films draw attention to the kinds of violence that are *not* directly represented.

Vol. 2 changes the presentation of Bill, moving away from the emphasis on mystery in the first film. *Vol. 1* never shows Bill's face, his hands are glimpsed wiping the blood from Beatrix's face and handling his Hanso sword when instructing Elle to abort the assassination. The partial views construct him as a sinister variant of Charles Townsend from the television series *Charlie's Angels* (ABC, 1976–81). The second film directly references David Carradine's role as the Shaolin monk, Kwai Chang Caine, in the television series *Kung Fu* (ABC, 1972–75). Similarities include playing the wooden flute and proficiency at martial arts techniques; however, Carradine is cast against type in that Bill is not a spiritual or moral exemplar. Bill's admiring story of Pai Mei's massacre of sixty Shaolin monks humorously indicates that his allegiances are different from Caine's, while also showing that he takes up martial arts purely as a means of eliminating the competition. Both Pai Mei and Esteban Vihaio are positioned as father figures to Bill, and both operate as extreme models of patriarchal power: Pai Mei's brutal tutelage involves total submission from the acolyte and Esteban's wealth rests on the sexual exploitation and violent subjugation of women. The second film thus positions Beatrix in relation to a series of patriarchal figures, each more brutal than the last. Indeed, her visit to Esteban at the beginning of the final chapter positions Bill's punishment, shooting her in the head, alongside Esteban's disfigurement of an unruly prostitute, in an endeavour to reconstruct the former as a loving gesture.

The circling structure of the second film, and its reflexive reconstruction of past events, is also explored through Bill's dialogue during the final encounter with Beatrix. Drawing on the discourses of nature, Bill argues that Beatrix is a 'natural born killer' and 'a renegade killer bee', reconstructing her professional role as an assassin as natural. This reconstruction goes against the second film's presentation of the lengthy and brutal training Beatrix endures, which suggests the reverse: she was not born an assassin but became one. As proof of his argument, Bill asks: 'All those people you killed to get to me ... felt good didn't it?' and Beatrix, under the influence of the truth drug, wrenchingly admits that this was the case. The exchange is interesting because it invites the spectator to re/view the battles at the end of *Vol. 1*, re/reading them as expressive of Beatrix's own pathology (as a natural born killer). This psychological explanation of the battles can only be accepted insofar as the viewer is prepared to forget the reflexive revelry of their presentation. In proffering a psychological reading that is directly counter to the first film's postmodern parody of screen violence, the dialogue foregrounds an unresolvable clash of perspectives, forcing the spectator to choose between the rewriting of the past in *Vol. 2* and their own memories of *Vol. 1*.

If Bill's interrogation marks a surprising return to the discourses of pop psychology, Beatrix's explanation of why she left him evokes equally unexpected discourses concerning the sanctity of human life. The film cuts to a flashback of Beatrix's positive pregnancy test and the subsequent encounter with female assassin, Karen. Beatrix appeals to Karen during the ensuing face-off, saying: 'I'm the deadliest woman in the world; right now I'm just scared shitless for my baby. Please, just look at the strip. Please.' The lines present the roles of assassin and mother as entirely oppositional: death-dealing and invincible versus life-giving and vulnerable. Beatrix's willingness to plead forms a marked contrast to her stony silence in other life-threatening situations, most notably during the encounter with Budd. Having grappled with the intricacies of reading the pregnancy test, Karen decides to abandon her mission, exiting the hotel room shouting: 'Congratulations!' through the hole she blasted in the door. The unborn child, metonymically represented by the positive pregnancy test, facilitates the positive resolution of the face-off. The figure of future life enables the two female assassins to choose life, a resolution that is entirely contrary to the carnage following the three-way face off at the end of *Reservoir*

Dogs (Quentin Tarantino, 1992). The unexpected utilisation of Catholic discourses concerning the foetus's right to life in the midst of a face-off offers a moment of complicitous critique in which a profoundly traditional conception of the maternal is both reinstated and rendered comic through its juxtaposition with radically different forms of femininity.

Kill Bill parallels Beatrix's first and last moments of revenge. The preliminary discussions with Vernita and Bill evoke images of battles that never happen, which are supposed to take place outside the domestic home, the baseball diamond and the beach respectively. Beatrix kills both antagonists in an immediate response to an unexpected attack, which utilises her training. However, the killing of Bill through the deployment of Pai Mei's exploding heart technique allows the pair of them time for reflection, enabling Bill to take his leave and Beatrix to fully realise the emotional cost of his death. The expansion of time marks a return to the exchange of formalities that structure the final duel in *Vol. 1*, O-Ren's apology replaced by Bill's warped benediction: 'No, you're not a bad person. You're a terrific person, you're my favourite person. But every once in a while you can be a complete cunt.' The formality of Bill's death is underscored by the use of Morricone's theme 'The Demise of Barbara and the Return of Joe' from *Navajo Joe* (Sergio Corbucci, 1966), the flurrying guitar riffs accompanying their final exchanges. Bill rises in accordance with the shift of orchestration, the chanting wail of the chorus accompanying his last five steps, falling down dead as the music stops. Carradine's last walk, barefoot across the grass to the Indian-style chanting, strongly recalls his Caine persona, granting Bill an almost benign authenticity in the moment of his death.

The structure of revenge in the second film circles back in on itself – killer and victim belong to the same family unit, marking a key shift from the spaghetti western to Greek tragedy. This shift is reflected in the plight of the children, Nicky and B.B., in the first and last scenes. Removing her knife from Vernita's body, Beatrix offers Nicky the chance of growing up to avenge her mother's death at the hands of a mysterious stranger: 'come lookin' for me and I'll be waitin''. In contrast, B.B. does not see the dead body of her father, or indeed know that her mother is his killer. B.B.'s fate will be that of Electra and Orestes, children who had to avenge the murder of their father by conspiring to kill/killing their mother. The unresolvable problematic of avenging the murder of blood kin through the murder of blood kin is part of the story of Orestes who murders his mother in accordance with Apollo's commands only to be pursued by the Furies.

The generic shift is accompanied by changes to the discourses of femininity used in relation to the female hero across *Vol. 1* and *Vol. 2*. The first film offers a complicitous critique of the consumptive sublime, drawing on its vision of feminine beauty in order to construct a spectacle of death and passivity, which the hero repeatedly overcomes. The consumptive sublime is thus utilised to form a new iconography for the female hero, paralleling the deployment of the tropes of crucifixion and martyrdom from high art in the presentation of the male hero (see Tasker 1993; Dyer 1997). *Vol. 2* can be seen to break away from the consumptive sublime in its presentation of the female hero being buried alive. The moment at which the screen goes black is both expressive of Beatrix's resolve and a complete break from a visual aesthetic that equates femininity, passivity and death.

Vol. 2 utilises the discourses of the maternal to construct a series of scenarios of conflicting obligations. Like Martha from *The Searchers*, Beatrix hovers at a threshold, pulled between very different loyalties: her lover versus her unborn child, professionalism versus motherhood, and danger versus domesticity. The foregrounding of contradiction in the presentation of Beatrix's absolutely incompatible identities greatly unsettles any attempt at a single definition. Bill's dialogue evokes Nature to argue that Beatrix is really a killer bee. The film itself closes the coda ending with a final image of Beatrix and B.B. smiling at the television together, followed by the inter-title: 'the lioness has rejoined her cub and all is right in the jungle'. This evocation of Nature confirms the bond between mother and child and marks the restoration of order; however, all the natural parallels simply demonstrate the incompatibility of Beatrix's roles: black mamba, killer bee and lioness. The torsions of *Vol. 2* – the contradictions of the mother/assassin and victim/avenger whose return marks the tragic rupturing of the domestic space – foreground the representational and conceptual difficulties of constructing a female hero who is also a mother.

The coda ending draws attention to its status as a complete impasse. The close-up of Beatrix's face as she succumbs to hysteria (the side effect of the truth drug) while lying on the bathroom floor, displays the emotional equivocalness of the ending, while also, as Gallafent notes, reverting to the formal structure of focusing on the star's face (2006: 120). The contrast between Thurman and Dietrich becomes most obvious at this point. *The Scarlet Empress* provides the spectacle of Sophia becoming the Empress

Catherine, which is also the process of becoming Dietrich, the ending constituting the final integration of screen role, performance and star persona. The close-up of Thurman's face shows her restless movement and shifts of expression in marked contrast to the stillness of *Vol. 1*. However, neither can be privileged in terms of star persona or performance. Instead the star moment showcases the transient mutability of fleeting expressions, displaying the intersection of a myriad of identities. *Vol. 2* cuts from the final intertitle to the credit sequence, displaying scenes from *Vol. 1*, as if Beatrix and B.B.'s story were unimaginable, reflecting the impasse presented by the Gordian knot of the revenge structure. The abrupt shift back to *Vol. 1* highlights the tonal differences between both films, pitting the reflexive postmodern parody of the final battles against the foregrounding of contradiction that paralyses the second. Importantly, it draws attention to the incompatibility of the films' perspectives, their very different meditations on the history of representation and screen violence. *Vol. 2* is not the last word on the significance of *Vol. 1*, evident from Esteban's and Bill's unsuccessful endeavours to rewrite the past, indeed through the credits, *Vol. 1* provides a release from the torsions and containment of *Vol. 2*.

CONCLUSION

As noted in chapter one, postmodern theorising does not slot neatly into place alongside previous systems. It does not leave everything as it was. Taking the challenges provided by Jean-François Lyotard and Linda Hutcheon seriously involves rethinking the aesthetic paradigms used to analyse Hollywood cinema, and the first chapter sets out a specific purview for the classical, post-classical and postmodern. While lack of space has prohibited further discussion of the post-classical, this book does delineate an affirmative postmodern aesthetic and realises some of its productive possibilities. On a Lyotardian model there is no such thing as a belated take up of postmodern theorising for Film Studies – the 'post-' is always with us – and indeed films such as *The Lego Movie* (Phil Lord and Christopher Miller, 2014) attest to its continual bubbling up in the present day.

The postmodern reader uses a wealth of different types of literacies in order to read the postmodern film text. These competencies vary from reader to reader, and thus the film readings offered at the end of chapter three attest to my own interests in Sherlock Holmes, female stars of the 1930s and spaghetti westerns. It is clear that silent cinema and studio-era cinema offer films that abound in intertextual references, including works of literature, plays, media interviews, magazines, as well as other films. Appreciating the bubbling up of the postmodern involves tracing intertexts and seeing the ways in which they intersect and interact with the film's narrative and characterisation, underscoring or undermining it, or telling yet another story.

Kill Bill deploys a range of references to very different effects. Fleeting instances, such as the reference to De Palma's *Carrie* as Beatrix rises from the grave of Paula Schulz, provide the pleasure of recognition and, in this particular case, a very welcome change of tone. The films repeatedly position the female hero in relation to her male predecessors – from Beatrix's surpassing of Bruce Lee at the end of *Vol. 1* to her failure to imitate Clint Eastwood in *Vol. 2* – thereby offering a sustained critical engagement with a history of representation. Dismissing the tracing of intertexts as the provision of self-congratulatory moments for the audience is disastrous because it forecloses the possibility of understanding the varied and the complex ways in which they can function across a postmodern text.

Both *Bombshell* and *Kill Bill* offer ways of rethinking the postmodern as a play of surfaces. Jean Harlow's performance as Lola offers a series of roles, some of which are more theatrical than others, thereby creating moments of authenticity. Bill's fleeting construction as (almost) benign at the point of death is a moment of integrity created by an intersection of intertexts, namely, Morricone's music and Carradine's previous roles. Both characters demonstrate the ways in which particular plays of surfaces can intersect and overlap, creating different constructions of depth. This marks a shift away from viewing the surface as merely superficial to the recognition of the potential integrity offered by plays of surfaces.

In addition to bringing their own range of literacies to a text, the postmodern spectator explicitly acknowledges the processes of selection and interpretation involved in creating a reading. *Kill Bill* draws attention to these processes by offering two very different films that circle back on each other, setting up incompatible perspectives on the past. Bill's reading of the final battles in *Vol. 1* as symptomatic of Beatrix's pathology, forces any spectator who enjoyed them to confront directly the differences between this reading of the violence and their own. Choosing between incompatible perspectives ensures the spectator begins to articulate their investment in viewing in a particular way, from a particular perspective, which is then reaffirmed by the reprisal of the battles in the final credits.

All the films discussed in the last part of chapter three offer moments of complicitous critique. The finale of *Sherlock Junior* both reinscribes and comically calls into question the mimetic model of film spectatorship. *Bombshell*'s parody of the Christian vision of motherhood is immediately followed by the reassertion of a traditional binary in the form of mother versus 'It girl'; however, the critique offered by the parody is not lost. Hutcheon argues that complicity cannot be used to cancel out moments of subversion: postmodern parody is 'complicitous with the values it inscribes as well as subverts, but the subversion is still there' (1989: 106). Thus, *Kill Bill* deploys the consumptive sublime, drawing on its equation of femininity, beauty and extreme passivity, in order to subvert it by repeatedly staging the spectacle of the female hero overcoming death. In this case, complicitous critique creates a new iconography for the female hero.

Hutcheon's assertion that 'the subversion is still there' (ibid.) draws attention to a key issue, namely the theorist's, and by extension the spectator's, investment in holding on to moments of critique. It is at this point that the project of postmodern reading is linked to questions of value and, indeed, to the political. The equivocal nature of the postmodern text means that choosing to hold open the possibility of complicitous critique is a political gesture. It is here that the issue of interpretation becomes a question of individual responsibility – taking responsibility for the willing of a perspective that is created through selection and interpretation. This is the final move beyond nihilism, in which the postmodern simply marks the end of ethics and all value. An affirmative postmodernism recognises that the values your interpretations help to create and sustain flow outwards into the wider world, while, in turn, delimiting what it is that you are and can become. There's a lot at stake in serious play.

BIBLIOGRAPHY

Allen, Michael (2003) *Contemporary US Cinema*. Harlow: Longman.

Balio, Tino (ed.) (1985a) *The American Film Industry*. Madison, WS: University of Wisconsin Press.

____ ([1976] 1985b) 'Part IV: Retrenchment, Reappraisal, and Reorganisation, 1948–', in Tino Balio (ed.) *The American Film Industry*. Madison, WS: University of Wisconsin Press, 401–47.

Barnes, Alan (2002) *Sherlock Holmes on Screen: The Complete Film and TV History*. London: Reynolds and Hearn.

Baron, Cynthia (1998) 'The Player's Parody of Hollywood: A Different Kind of Suture', in Cristina Degli-Esposti (ed.) *Postmodernism in the Cinema*. New York: Berghahn, 21–43.

Baudrillard, Jean (1983) *Simulations*, trans. Paul Foss, Paul Patton and Phillip Beitchman. New York: Semiotext(e).

____ (1988) *America*, trans. Chris Turner. New York and London: Verso.

____ (1994) *Simulacra and Simulations*, trans. Shelia Faria Glaser. Ann Arbor, MI: University of Michigan Press.

Boggs, Carl and Tom Pollard (2003) *A World in Chaos: Social Crisis and the Rise of Postmodern Cinema*. New York and Oxford: Rowman and Littlefield.

Booker, M. Keith (2007) *Postmodern Hollywood: What's New in Film and Why It Makes Us Feel So Strange*. London: Praeger.

Bordwell, David (1985) 'Part One: The classical Hollywood style 1917–60', in David Bordwell, Janet Staiger and Kristin Thompson, *The Classical Hollywood Cinema: Film Style and Mode of Production to 1960*. London: Routledge and Kegan Paul, 1–84.

____ (2006) *The Way Hollywood Tells It: Story and Style in Modern Movies*. Berkeley, CA: University of California Press.

Bordwell, David, Janet Staiger and Kristin Thompson (1985) *The Classical Hollywood Cinema: Film Style and Mode of Production to 1960*. London: Routledge and Kegan Paul.

Brooker, Peter and Will Brooker (eds) (1997a) *Postmodern After-Images: A Reader in Film, Television and Video*. London: Arnold.

_____ (1997b) 'Pulpmodernism: Tarantino's affirmative action', in Peter Brooker and Will Brooker (eds) *Postmodern After-Images: A Reader in Film, Television and Video*. London: Arnold, 89–100.

Cahoone, Lawrence (1996) *From Modernism to Postmodernism*. Oxford and Cambridge, MA: Blackwell.

Carr, S. A. (2000) 'From "Fucking Cops" to "Fucking Media": *Bonnie and Clyde* for a Sixties America', in Lester D. Friedman (ed.) *Arthur Penn's Bonnie and Clyde*. Cambridge: Cambridge University Press, 70–100.

Carroll, Nöel (1982) 'The Future of Allusion: Hollywood in the Seventies and Beyond', *October*, 20, 20, 51–81.

Charbonnier, C. (1993) 'I like the cinema', in Mike Gane (ed.) *Baudrillard Live: Selected Interviews*, trans. M. Gane and G. Salemohamed. London and New York: Routledge, 29–35.

Clover, Carol J. (1992) *Men, Women and Chainsaws: Gender in the Modern Horror Film*. Princeton, NJ: Princeton University Press.

Collins, Jim (1989) *Uncommon Cultures: Popular Cultures and Postmodernism*. New York and London: Routledge.

Collins, Jim, Hilary Radner and Ava Preacher Collins (eds) (1993) *Film Theory Goes to the Movies*. London: Routledge.

Conan-Doyle, Sir Arthur (1887) *A Study in Scarlet*. London: Ward and Lock.

Constable, Catherine (2005) *Thinking in Images: Film Theory, Feminist Philosophy and Marlene Dietrich*. London: British Film Institute.

_____ (2009a) *Adapting Philosophy: Jean Baudrillard and The Matrix Trilogy*. Manchester: Manchester University Press.

_____ (2009b) 'Jean Baudrillard', in Felicity Colman (ed.) *Film, Theory and Philosophy: The Key Thinkers*. Durham: Acumen, 212–21.

_____ (2009c) 'Reflections on the Surface: Remaking the Postmodern with van Sant's *Psycho*', in Rachel Carroll (ed.) *Adaptation in Contemporary Culture: Textual Infidelities*. London and New York: Continuum, 23–33.

_____ (2014) 'Postmodern Cinema', in Edward Branigan and Warren Buckland (eds) *The Routledge Encyclopedia of Film Theory*. London and New York: Routledge, 376–83.

Davies, Dentner (1937) *Jean Harlow: Hollywood Comet*. London: Constable.

De Boer, Jason (2005) 'The Fatal "Theory-Fiction" of Jean Baudrillard', *International Journal of Baudrillard Studies*, 2, 1, 1–5.

De Cordova, Richard (1991) 'The Emergence of the Star System in America', Christine Gledhill (ed.) *Stardom: Industry of Desire*. New York and London: Routledge, 17–29.

Degli-Esposti, Cristina (ed.) (1998a) *Postmodernism in the Cinema*. New York: Berghahn.

____ (1998b) 'Introduction: Postmodernism(s)', in Cristina Degli-Esposti (ed.) *Postmodernism in the Cinema*. New York: Berghahn, 3–18.

Denzin, Norman K. (1991) *Images of Postmodern Society: Social Theory and Contemporary Cinema*. Newbury Park, CA/London: Sage.

____ (1995) *The Cinematic Society: The Voyeur's Gaze*. Thousand Oaks, CA/London: Sage.

Dijkstra, Bram (1986) *Idols of Perversity: Fantasies of Feminine Evil in Fin-de-Siècle Culture*. Oxford and New York: Oxford University Press.

Dika, Vera (2003) *Recycled Culture in Contemporary Art and Film: The Uses of Nostalgia*. Cambridge: Cambridge University Press.

Doane Mary Ann (1991) *Femmes Fatales: Feminism, Film Theory and Psychoanalysis*. New York and London: Routledge.

Docherty, Thomas (ed.) (1993) *Postmodernism: A Reader*. New York and London: Harvester Wheatsheaf.

Dyer, Richard (1979) *Stars*. London: British Film Institute.

____ (1997) *White*. London and New York: Routledge.

____ (2007) *Pastiche*. London and New York: Routledge.

Elsaesser, Thomas and Warren Buckland (2002) *Studying Contemporary American Film: A Guide to Movie Analysis*. London: Arnold.

Gallafent, Edward (2006) *Quentin Tarantino*. Harlow: Pearson Education.

Gane, Mike (ed.) (1993) *Baudrillard Live: Selected Interviews*, trans. M. Gane and G. Salemohamed. London and New York: Routledge.

Garrett, Roberta (2007) *Postmodern Chick Flicks: The Return of the Woman's Film*. Basingstoke: Palgrave Macmillan.

Gledhill, Christine and Linda Williams (eds) (2000) *Reinventing Film Studies*. London: Arnold.

Goethe, Johann Wolfgang ([1828–29; 1832] 1999) *Faust: A Tragedy in Two Parts and The Urfaust*. Ware: Wordsworth Editions.

Hall, Sheldon (2002) 'Tall Revenue Features: The Genealogy of the Modern Blockbuster', in Steve Neale (ed.) *Genre and Contemporary Hollywood*. London: British Film Institute, 11–26.

_____ (2008) Unpublished lecture on the blockbuster delivered at the University of Warwick, 23 January.

Hanley, Richard (2003) 'Simulacra and Simulation: Baudrillard and *The Matrix*'; Available at: http//whatisthematrix.warnerbros.com (accessed 3 March 2004).

Hansen, Miriam Bratu (2000) 'The Mass Production of the Senses: Classical Cinema as Vernacular Modernism', in Christine Gledhill and Linda Williams (eds) *Reinventing Film Studies*. London: Arnold, 332–50.

Hill, John (1998) 'Film and Postmodernism', in John Hill and Pamela Church Gibson (eds) *The Oxford Guide to Film Studies*. Oxford: Oxford University Press, 96–105.

Hill, John and Pamela Church Gibson (eds) (1998) *The Oxford Guide to Film Studies*. Oxford: Oxford University Press.

Hutcheon, Linda (1988) *A Poetics of Postmodernism: History, Theory, Fiction*. New York and London: Routledge.

_____ (1989) *The Politics of Postmodernism*. New York and London: Routledge.

Jameson, Frederic (1983) 'Postmodernism and Consumer Society', in Hal Foster (ed.) *The Anti-Aesthetic: Essays on Postmodern Culture*. Seattle, WA: Bay Press, 111–25.

_____ (1991) *Postmodernism, or, The Cultural Logic of Late Capitalism*. London: Verso.

Jordan, Jessica Hope (2009) *The Sex Goddess in American Film 1930–1965*. Amherst, MA: Cambria Press.

Kaplan, E. Ann (1987) *Rocking Around the Clock: Music Television, Postmodernism, and Consumer Culture*. London: Methuen.

King, Geoff (2000) *Spectacular Narratives: Hollywood in the Age of the Blockbuster*. London: I.B. Tauris.

_____ (2002a) *Film Comedy*. London and New York: Wallflower Press.

_____ (2002b) *New Hollywood Cinema: An Introduction*. London: I.B. Tauris.

Kofman, Sarah (1988) 'Baubô: Theological Perversion and Fetishism', trans. Tracey B. Strong, in Michael Allen Gillespie and Tracey B. Strong (eds) *Nietzsche's New Seas: Explorations in Philosophy, Aesthetics and Politics*. Chicago: University of Chicago Press, 175–202.

Krämer, Peter (1998) 'Post-classical Hollywood', in John Hill and Pamela Church Gibson (eds) *The Oxford Guide to Film Studies*. Oxford: Oxford University Press, 289–309.

____ (2005) *The New Hollywood: From Bonnie and Clyde to Star Wars*. London and New York: Wallflower Press.

Leroux, Gaston (1911) *The Phantom of the Opera*. Paris: Pierre Lafitte and Cie.

Lyotard, Jean-François (1984a) *The Postmodern Condition: A Report on Knowledge*, trans. G. Bennington and B. Massumi. Manchester: Manchester University Press.

____ (1984b) 'Answering the Question: What Is Postmodernism?', in *The Postmodern Condition: A Report on Knowledge*, trans. G. Bennington and B. Massumi. Manchester: Manchester University Press, 71–82.

____ (1992) 'Notes on the Meaning of "Post-"', in *The Postmodern Explained to Children: Correspondence 1982–1985*, trans. D. Barry, B. Maher, J. Perfanis, V. Spate and M. Thomas. London: Turnaround, 87–93.

MacDonald, Paul (2000) *The Star System: Hollywood's Production of Popular Identities*. London and New York: Wallflower Press.

Marx, Karl (1867) *Capital, Volume One*; available at http://www.marxists.org/archive/marx/works/1867-c1/ch01.htm (accessed 25 January 2011).

Merrin, William (2005) *Baudrillard and the Media*. Cambridge: Polity Press.

Neale, Steve (ed.) (2002) *Genre and Contemporary Hollywood*. London: British Film Institute.

Neale, Steve and Murray Smith (eds) (1998) *Contemporary Hollywood Cinema*. London: Routledge.

Nietzsche, Friedrich ([1892] 1982) *Thus Spoke Zarathustra*, in *The Portable Nietzsche*, trans. and ed. Walter Kaufmann. New York and London: Viking Penguin, 103–439.

Ohmer, Susan (2011) 'Jean Harlow: Tragic Blonde', in Adrienne L. McLean (ed.) *Glamour in a Golden Age: Movie Stars of the 1930s*. New Brunswick, NJ: Rutgers University Press.

Pirie, David (ed.) (1981a) *Anatomy of the Movies*. London: Windward.

____ (1981b) 'The Deal', in David Pirie (ed.) *Anatomy of the Movies*. London: Windward, 40–61.

Schatz, Thomas (1993) 'The New Hollywood', in Jim Collins, Hilary Radner and Ava Preacher Collins (eds) *Film Theory Goes to the Movies*. New York: Routledge, 8–36.

Shary, Timothy (1998) 'Reification and Loss in Postmodern Puberty: The Cultural Logic of Frederic Jameson and American Youth Movies', in Cristina Degli-Esposti (ed.) *Postmodernism in the Cinema*. New York: Berghahn, 73–91.

Staiger, Janet (1985) 'Part Two: The Hollywood mode of production, 1930–1960', in David Bordwell, Janet Staiger and Kristin Thompson, *The Classical Hollywood Cinema: Film Style and Mode of Production to 1960*. London: Routledge and Kegan Paul, 309–37.

Tasker, Yvonne (1993) *Spectacular Bodies: Gender, Genre and the Action Cinema*. London and New York: Routledge.

Thomas, Deborah (1990) 'Blonde Venus (1932)', *Movie*, 34/35, Winter, 7–15.

Thompson, Kristin (1999) *Storytelling in the New Hollywood: Understanding Classical Narrative Technique*. Cambridge, MA: Harvard University Press.

Wilde, Oscar ([1891] 1992) *The Picture of Dorian Gray*. Ware: Wordsworth Editions.

Williams, Linda (2000) 'Discipline and Fun: Psycho and Postmodern Cinema', in Christine Gledhill and Linda Williams (eds) *Reinventing Film Studies*. London: Arnold, 351–78.

INDEX